THE BALTIC STATES IN
WORLD POLITICS

THE BALTIC STATES IN WORLD POLITICS

Edited by
Birthe Hansen
and
Bertel Heurlin

St. Martin's Press
New York

Copyright © 1998 by Bertel Heurlin and Birthe Hansen

All rights reserved. No part of this book may be used or
reproduced in any manner whatsoever without written permission
except in the case of brief quotations embodied in critical articles
or reviews. For information, address:

St. Martin's Press, Scholarly and Reference Division,
175 Fifth Avenue, New York, N.Y. 10010

First published in the United States of America in 1998
Printed in Great Britain

ISBN 0–312–21526–6
ISBN 0–312–21527–4

Library of Congress Cataloging in Publication Data

The Baltic states in world politics/edited by Birthe Hansen and
Bertel Heurlin.
p. cm.
Includes bibliographical references and index
ISBN 0–312–21526–6 (cloth). – ISBN 0–312–21527–4 (pbk.)
1. Baltic States–Foreign relations. I. Hansen, Birthe.
II. Heurlin, Bertel.
JZ1628.B35 1998
947.908'6–dc21   98–16502
CIP

Contents

Introduction

Birthe Hansen and Bertel Heurlin

The aim of this collaborative work has been to focus on the international dimension of Estonia's, Latvia's and Lithuania's security challenges after their re-emergence as independent states in the late Summer of 1991. With the re-emergence of the three Baltic States providing International Politics with new cases, as well as subjecting each to the changed general dynamics of the international system, it has also been our intent to apply concepts from the discipline of 'International Politics' to their security challenges. Moreover, with the international dimension having turned global in its perspective, the Baltic States' regional opportunities are at once strongly connected with the post-1989 shaping of patterns of conflict and co-operation, as well as with the strategic approach of the United States. It has therefore been considered imperative that an analysis of the Baltics' security situation assume not only a national or regional context, but a global political perspective as well.

The period from 1991 onwards has been characterised by several dramatic international changes. Although the independence of the Baltic States ranks among these changes, the states themselves have also been deeply affected by changes arising out of their efforts to consolidate and improve their international position. Thus, with the international system still in the throes of a transformation process following the end of the Cold War, the analytical object under observation here is quite naturally a slippery one. Subsequently, one means by which an understanding can be maintained is by the use of 'conceptualisation'.

In the Baltics' most relevant sphere, one can clearly see that the European Union is enlarging, that NATO has decided to enlarge, and that Russia is struggling to adapt to a new international role. Seen within these historic processes, the Baltic States are merely small units dependent upon decisions taken far from their own capitals. Given their specific geopolitical positioning between the 'old West' and Russia, however, they are subjected to a particularly acute attention in spite of their smallness. As a result, they have come to represent incarnations of several post-Cold War dilemmas including:

- What are the new limits of the West?
- How does Russia respond to the international changes?
- And does the 'new' Europe extend to include even parts of the former Soviet Union?

In addition to the political questions, theoretical questions arise:

- How do small states seceding from a losing, collapsing empire react when exposed to a new international context?
- Do the Baltic States and their counterparts act according to the general theoretical statement on international alignment?
- And what, in fact, does their international position tell us about the new World Order?

Though these are the broad fundamental questions which inspire this volume, they are modest in relation to the daunting challenge of answering them. However, in presenting the following seven chapters based on classic theoretical concepts, the goal here is to provide a preliminary view on the combination of the Baltic States' re-emergence and the changing international system. Taken together, these chapters represent a concept-related analysis of different viewpoints regarding the Baltic security environment linked by the international dimension.

Mare Haab assesses the Baltic States' potentials for coping with the international challenges. She analyses the potentials of the three states as well as their vulnerabilities. Her analysis brings about an assessment covering the features of both internal and external factors, and highlights the dimension of political competence and stability.

Peter van Ham analyses both the Baltic States and the major Western institutions in order to reveal the interplay between the spread of these institutions and the Baltics' adaptation to the 'new' Europe. The chapter goes on to offer a survey of the Baltics' actual affiliations, memberships and positions.

Stuart Kaufman addresses the security dilemma from the origins of the West's attempts to secure its position as well as from the Baltic perspective of NATO enlargement. In their effects upon Russia, the dilemma is dealt with from the position of all three sides. The chapter places special emphasis on the American policy towards the Baltic States by isolating the different tendencies within the US establishment.

Bertel Heurlin focuses on the interplay between the transformation of NATO and the security dilemma. He analyses the effect of the transformation process upon Russia and, in so doing, the very nature of the issue for the Baltic States positioned between Russia and the West. Correspondingly, he also examines the development of the new security agenda.

Birthe Hansen applies a neorealist model of unipolarity to the Baltic States' adaptation to new security challenges. She analyses both the long-term challenges of alignment as well as the corresponding security strategies available. In addition, she offers a discussion on the conditions of small states in the post-Cold War international order.

Lena Jonson addresses the Russian policy towards the 'near abroad'. The pivotal analytical perspective is the compatibility between Russian ambitions and Russian capabilities, with the findings concluding that a broad gap exists between Moscow's declaratory positions and its actual political approach.

Alexander Pikayev summarises the historical record of alignments and security challenges in the Baltic Sea region in order to highlight the continuing as well as changing patterns, and consequently, to identify the degree of sensitivity of various factors to international transformation.

In choosing different theoretical points of departure, the authors notably do not agree on the prospects for Baltic security.

In the Autumn of 1996, the Danish Institute of International Affairs (DUPI) convened an academic conference on the Baltics entitled, 'The Baltic States in World Politics'. The chapters in this volume represent elaborated versions of papers read and discussed at the conference.[1]

February 1997

---

[1] The editors would like to thank graduate student of Political Science, Jess Pilegaard, DUPI, for providing invaluable help with preparing the manuscript.

Chapter 1

Potentials and vulnerabilities of the Baltic States

Mutual competition and cooperation

Mare Haab

Introduction

The plural form 'the Baltics' entered into international political discourse more frequently at the close of the 1980s. Political changes occurring in Eastern and Central Europe leading to the collapse of the coalition of the Warsaw Pact states, the reunification of Germany and the subsequent dissolution of the Soviet Union, made it possible for the Baltic countries to regain their independence and thus restore the primary conditions for their international action and interaction. Overall changes in the 'power constellation' of World politics – with the end of bipolarity – explicitly suggested the emergence of a new security architecture in Europe. Subsequently, the three Baltic countries of Estonia, Latvia and Lithuania found themselves provided with the realistic opportunity to be part of this new arrangement.

Upon entering into a manoeuvrable position previously unavailable since the 1940 Soviet occupation, the Baltics' scale of options for international identification has become seemingly broad, ranging from a position as "bridge" between East and West to multiple forms of regional and continental alliances. However, due to a lack of any solid experience in international relations or the prerequisite instruments of policy-making, the three countries face the extremely complex task of determining the most appropriate geopolitical strategies vis-à-vis the dynamic, evolving processes of the European core organisations – the European Community (EC) and the North Atlantic Treaty Organisation (NATO).

The 1991 international recognition of Estonia, Latvia and Lithuania's regained independence, which initiated a relatively similar state-building process to its earlier period, was affected by two

1

dominant factors: firstly, since the basis for the restoration of their independence was the principle of 'historical legal continuity', inputs from historical memory associated with the 1918–1940 independence – and amplified by strong anti-Soviet (anti-Russian) sentiment – played the essential role in this regard. This political stand, together with the related prevailing emotions, suggested restoration of the pre-war legislations, state institutions and policy-making mechanisms; secondly, contemporary Western models of co-operation exercised on the level of the Nordic countries, the EU and NATO, for the Baltic countries marked the case of stable relations between economically wealthy and militarily secure states, thus providing the most admirable model to be achieved. These two basic factors have significantly influenced the way the Baltics conduct their own policies in relation to their new international role and, subsequently, have considerably affected the notion of Baltic unity as well.

This chapter attempts to reflect upon the basic determinants which have either hampered or favoured the subregional co-operation and integration of the three Baltic States; to this end, it will also evaluate their potentials and vulnerabilities as well. The purpose here is to point out the principle internal and external factors which affect the formulation of the security and defence policies in Estonia, Latvia and Lithuania. Subsequently, special emphasis will be placed on the politico-military aspect of security. In addition, each Baltic country's prospects in the theatre of World politics, along with the question of whether the three 'seemingly alike' states possess sufficient features in common to provide for the establishment of a sustainable and well-functioning subregional entity will be addressed.

Pre-independence Baltic unity: symbolic in form, strategic in essence

At the end of the 1980s the Baltic countries entered a period of openly striving for a common goal – the restoration of independence. Small and weak in terms of size and capability, as well as situated on a territory of great importance to their immediate big neighbour, Russia, it was extremely obvious that the three closely located, Soviet occupied republics used the form of united efforts to increase their potentials and perform co-ordinated activities against the central powers of the Soviet Union. The establishment of the Popular Fronts in 1988 (first in Estonia and thereafter in Latvia and Lithuania[1]) paved the way for the peaceful mass activities which conveyed the spirit of national liberation.

Thus, in August 1989, the highly emotional picture depicting the chain of hundreds of thousands of Estonians, Latvians and Lithuanians standing side by side and forwarding from Tallinn to Vilnius the password "freedom", foretold the ultimate desire of the Baltic people. The almost theatrical expression of their common political aspirations became the hallmark of pre-independence Baltic unity and significantly contributed to the external perception that the three countries acted as a singular political unit. Given their limited political means, it also served as the most effective political strategy to signal their existence to the international community; correspondingly, it ensured the morally supportive bearing of the Western community.

The highly similar political and economic conditions of the three Baltic republics, along with the similar nature of their relations with the external political environment, account for the joint efforts to separate themselves politically from the Soviet Union. In all three countries, the initial movement towards economic autonomy from the USSR was complimented by the idea of Baltic neutrality.[2] Neutrality was perceived as a credible argument in demanding the Soviet Union's withdrawal of numerous occupational troops from the Baltic territory. Both aspirations in the pre-independence period suggest that, at the very least, the Baltic republics were reluctant to become a "bridge" between the East and the West *for fear of becoming too attached to the West or diminishing the domain of the East.*

Beginning in 1990, initial attempts were made to add an institutionally-based 'practical' dimension to the existing emotional one in order to establish inter-governmental co-operation between the three countries. The aim was to create the common fora for articulating autonomous policies and for providing assistance "in the full restoration of state independence of the three Republics".[3] The need to strengthen political capability through subregional unity became further actuated by the resolutions on independence adopted by the Supreme Councils of Lithuania on March 11, Estonia on March 30 and Latvia on May 4, 1990. Thus, in May 1990, heads of the Baltic countries signed the Declaration of Concord and Co-operation, re-establishing also the Council of the Baltic States (founded in 1934).

Judging by the general character of events performed during their strive for independence, the primary factor inducing the Baltic countries to pool their resources and act in a unified manner was their common eastern neighbour. The aim was to explicitly advocate

Baltic solidarity against the big power of the East and thus increase the limited potentials of being considered independent entities by the international community.

Common threat perception: backbone of the official security and defence policies

While the Soviet Union lost the Cold War, Estonia, Latvia and Lithuania were on the side of the winners. Though the Baltic republics did not reap from the Soviet Union economically, politically, and least of all militarily, they did gain the opportunity to become independent and, therefore, were among the most rewarded. However, having been positioned on the 'forward-line' of heightened tension during the bipolar world order, from the Baltic perspective the Cold War's end – along with any explicitly new nature of the collapsed Soviet Union – was not seen as eminently as it was from a more distant point of view. The primary reason derives from the complex relationship between the Baltic States and the Soviet Union (later Russia).

Mistrust and fear towards Russia have been the commonly shared emotions among Balts. Heavy militarisation of the Baltic region during the Soviet period, along with the practised national policy of "Russification" by the central authorities of the USSR, considerably added to the anxieties among Estonians, Latvians and Lithuanians in the preservation of their national identities.[4] These same two emotions have also considerably shaped the security and defence policy understandings in all three Baltic states.

First and foremost, the withdrawal of Soviet troops prevailed as the most significant common concern in uniting the security policy principles of Estonia, Latvia and Lithuania. In addition to the popular manifestations and activities carried out on the level of the general public, this problem was the primary topic of the Baltic parliaments and governments in the early 90s. The inter-parliamentary Baltic Assembly, established on 8 November 1991, along with the Council of the Baltic States and regular meetings of the Baltic presidents, prime ministers and ministers of foreign affairs all largely became involved with the troops withdrawal issue. In order to solve the sensitive issue of Russia's military might, allied efforts appealing to the Western community were utilised to increase the capability of the small states.

Simultaneously, the idea of neutrality gradually lost meaning and credibility for the Balts due to several reasons. *First of all*, within the changing context of East-West relations, it became outdated in the international debate as the means for providing security. For the Baltic States signs became evident that the role of neutrality in a diminishing confrontation environment was no longer applicable. *Secondly,* neutrality was assumed to be synonymous with the bitter historical memories of the Baltic States' failed experience in the 1930s. *Thirdly,* neutrality was feared as an obstacle for Estonia, Latvia and Lithuania's westward integration and alliance policies of the future.[5] These arguments served as the most transparent explanations for what could be termed the Baltics' 'maximum choice' – full alignment with the West.

As NATO and the EU came to head a political rhetoric which emphasised the Baltics having had belonged to the European cultural-religious area since the 13the century and thus possessed of the right to be part of the continent's contemporary security and defence mechanisms as a logical continuation of their history, they thus became the only suitable entities for the Balts. Consequently similar to the rest of the Central and East European countries, the Baltic States already envisioned a future in each organization.

The Atlantic Alliance was perceived as the only existing mechanism capable of both countering the strivings of the USSR (and later Russia), and restoring its lost positions in the Baltics. Subregional inter-Baltic security and defence co-operation, without much credible substance or success in the inter-war period, was considered by all three countries to be an inadequate means of providing protection from external threats. The Nordic countries, though the most supportive countries in terms of Baltic independence, developed their own individual security and defence arrangements during the Cold War and, therefore, were not prepared to take defence responsibilities for any post-communist country. All security agreements with the Soviet Union and its successor, Russia, were excluded for political and psychological reasons. The prevailing threat-perception considered Russia to be the predominant source of external threat against each individual Baltic country, as well as all of them together. This argument has been strongly bound to historical prejudices and supported by certain tendencies disclosing themselves in post-Cold War Russian-Baltic relations:

First, mistrust towards Russia is rooted in the history of the Baltic countries. The interpretation of the occupation of Estonia, Latvia and Lithuania in 1940 places all follow-up consequences on the shoulders of the Soviet Union and its communist leadership. To the Baltic countries, Russia is still entirely identified with the Soviet Union. The primary reasons for this are connected to the fact that in purely judicial terms, as Russia became the legal successor to the Soviet Union with the creation of the Commonwealth of Independent States in December 1991, vis-à-vis the Baltic States it continued several features of the policy characteristic of the Soviet Union.

The first and foremost among these is Russia's expansionist ideology. Advocated not only as political rhetoric by some key Russian politicians[6], but also through numerous official and semi-official documents, this ideology, while determining the basis of the foreign and defence policies of the Russian Federation, does not convince the Baltic States of the "newness" of "new" Russia's identity. The "direct protection" of Russian-speaking minorities in the near-abroad countries who "culturally and ethnically identify themselves with the Russian Federation"[7] does not rule out scenarios restoring Great Russia through military means. From a Baltic perspective, since Russia has emphasised this as both a moral and legal basis for locating troops on Baltic territory[8], these scenarios would also directly affect Estonia, Latvia and Lithuania.

Second, Russia's rigid opposition to the dimensional development of NATO, particularly vis-à-vis the Baltic States, signals their viewing the international community still through the prism of 'spheres of influence' and thus marks the Baltic States as semi-sovereign satellites to Russia. Due to geographic proximity, this way of political thinking reveals the most transparent source of threat to the Balts' independent statehood. As a countermeasure to NATO enlargement in the direction of the Baltic countries, Russia has also regarded nuclear deployment in Kaliningrad, Belarus and the Norwegian-Russian border.[9] Such force- and threat-line tactics, characteristic of the Soviet Union, suggests to the Balts that it is still part of Russia's political identity and that the 'new' Russia is perfectly capable of "violently taking over the power in the state, possibly by means of peacekeeping forces to guarantee the security of their citizens".[10]

Third, Russia's political elite is comprised of a large number of the old Soviet Union's Communist Party ex-nomenclature (though a marginal faction of the democratic forces). Together with uneasiness among the Russian military, strikes, and discontent over the economic and social conditions in Russia on the part of society in general, for Lilian Shevtsova, political scientist from the Carnegi Centre in Moscow, this indicates that "the society is in deep stagnation".[11] As seen by their Baltic neighbours, Russia remains an unstable, unpredictable power closest in vicinity.

Though the Baltic countries' sensitivity to the movements and rhetoric of their geographically adjacent big power is understandably high, for Russia such actions frequently constitute the internal politics, election campaigns or peculiarities and hardships of the democratisation process. Nevertheless, Baltic fear derives not only from an uncertainty regarding the stability of their unexpectedly regained independent statehood, but also from concerns about the depth and extent of Western support.

Although the Western world never officially recognised the illegal Soviet annexation of the Baltic States from 1940–1991, their post-Second World War recognition of the western border of the Soviet Union indicated that the West had actually accepted the Baltic countries as being part of the Soviet Union. However, the post-bipolar world order promised an increased attention on the part of the West towards the security concerns of the Baltic countries; subsequently, the Balts, in seeking to acquire moral and practical support from the West since the restoration of their independence, have pursued a policy of 'internationalising their threat perception' and acquiring at least a politically secure distance from their potential source of danger by removing themselves from the Russian "sphere of influence".

This principle has become the commonly shared line in the security and defence policies of Estonia, Latvia and Lithuania. Correspondingly, the primary means to facilitate this has been to strive for inclusion in the Western institutional networks and become anchored to the core security organisations of Europe. Conversely, Russia, in providing the threat perception for the Baltic States, has indeed unintentionally contributed to Baltic unity.

From competing Atlantic alliance euphoria to constructive cooperation

'West is the best'

After the Baltic nations became generally recognised members of the international community, no explicit follow-up steps were taken towards greater Baltic unity. Quite to the contrary, each of the states became engaged in a number of independent activities including: conducting elections for their legislative bodies; forming respective governments; solving the questions connected with citizenship;

introducing reform policies; regulating the internal and external problems with respect to Russia; and indirectly aspiring to attract economic investments from the West. On the international level, they became strongly involved in such institutional activities as: joining the UN and the CSCE in September 1991; membership in the Council of the Baltic Sea States (CBSS) in March 1992; the North Atlantic Co-operation Council (NACC) in December 1992; the Council of Europe (CE) in Summer 1993; and status in the Associated Members of the West European Union (WEU) exactly one year later.

This complex institutional network served the Baltic States primarily as an efficient means to internationalise their security concerns. Depending upon the character of each concrete organisation, for Estonia, Latvia and Lithuania they either represented the fora for righting and overthrowing Russia's political accusations (UN, CSCE/ OSCE, CE), the expanded co-operation among Western democracies, or the enhanced competence and increased capability through consultations and discussions (CBSS, NACC, WEU). As a result of their associated partner status, access to the WEU Permanent Council discussions and the Planning Cell activities has increased the Baltic States' confidence in being acknowledged as integral parts of European security considerations. Thus, the numerous international organisa-tions, in being linked to issues of international stability and acting as confidence-building measures, have had a very definite impact on the peaceful state-building process in the Baltics.

However, for the Baltic politicians who consider the issue of national defence to be strongly associated with the notions of total defence, territorial defence and military means, none of these organisations have dealt directly with their highest concern – extending military security guarantees.[12] This issue has also been beyond the capability of the European pillar of NATO, the WEU, whose limited operational and budgetary means have failed to meet the security and defence needs of the restored Baltic States. Consequently, the Baltic countries have ranked among those states with strategic objectives for achieving NATO membership.

This aim, considerably reinforced by the euphoria and rhetoric which immediately followed the collapse of the Soviet Union, has also been voiced by NATO in its emphasis on the major role for the Alliance in the post-bipolar world order. Subsequently, NATO has not only been perceived by the Baltic authorities as the most efficient international security mechanism, but an organisation which would always maintain its defensive character and extend the benefits of common defence to all its members who shared the common values of peace, freedom and democracy.

Thus, achieving full membership in the Atlantic Alliance became the common concern for all three small states. The other key organisation in forming the basis for the foreign and security policies of the Baltic States, the European Union (EC initially), has been associated with the term "existential security" i.e., a means for establishing the economic and political conditions necessary for the increased well-being and stability of the people. However, Soviet President Mikhail Gorbachev's idea of a "common European house" in the early days of the Balts' independence made the identity and perspectives of this entity blurred in relation to that of NATO. Consequently, the Baltics' main emphasis was placed on fostering the NATO policy line.

These institutionally-determined objectives have triggered obvious competitions between Estonia, Latvia and Lithuania in their attempts to achieve their ultimate goals. It is here that these seemingly alike small states have chosen to focus on the differences rather than the common characteristics of their conditions. The main differences involve the ethnic composition and border problems of Estonia and Latvia, which are strongly related to Russia. *Lithuania*, however, with an ethnic Lithuanian population constituting approximately 80 per cent, has no internationally recognised minority problems. Additionally, it is void of border disputes with its major neighbouring states.[13] However, Russia's transit through Lithuania to Kaliningrad, which comprises an area of Russian state interest, adds a specific vulnerability to this Baltic State.

Latvia does not face any major problems with its mainland borders either. However, with an indigenous population comprising a little over one half of the total population in relation to approximately 34 per cent for Russians[14], there is grounds for argument vis-à-vis Russia. In addition, a military facility of Russia, the Skrunda radar station, is to function in Latvia until 1998 and thus presents a very concrete military-related vulnerability. *Estonia* also has a relatively large minority – it was roughly 38,5 per cent of the total population in 1989 and an estimated 32,6 per cent in 1996.[15] In addition, Estonia also has territorial problems deriving from the 1920 Tartu Peace Treaty with Russia. Hence, the different approach to the citizenship policy as well as the noticeable differences in the nature of relations between each of the Baltic States and Russia is easily comprehensible.

In terms of the speed and radicality with which reforms have been carried out, each state has been explicitly different. As a result, there has been a reluctance to take on the additional responsibilities and problems derived from being co-allies in a tightly interlinked Baltic entity. The logic has followed that a sub-regional alignment would mean voluntary acceptance on the part of each to lower their already modest level of capability, a move seen as subsequently increasing their vulnerability. Conversely, keeping out of the unity would serve to increase their individual capability and allow for more realistic perspectives to become included in strong Western alliances.

"Estonia maintains the highest level of stability in the sphere of legislative order and is the country with the most rapid economic development on the territory of the former Soviet Union", declared the Estonian President Lennart Meri in his Brussels speech to NATO on 25 November 1992.[16] On 4 January 1994 Lithuania became the first Baltic state to present the letter of the President as an official application of its membership to NATO. Thus, it has largely been the Baltics' common goals that have paved the way for certain rivalries and competitions between the states e.g., aspiring for hard (military) and soft (society-related) security guarantees from the Western organisations has kept them from establishing any distinct alliance.

Nato: from a distant dream to Baltic reality

Beginning in 1994, the NATO political line became more concrete for the Baltic States. This can be traced to the NATO Summit in January 1994 and to the Partnership for Peace (PfP) initiative. To the Baltic States, the NATO Summit declaration in paragraph twelve that "we expect and would welcome NATO expansion"[17], signalled the Alliance's receptivity to new members. For its part, the Partnership for Peace programme pointed the way to acquire NATO-required standards. This concrete proposal also effectively bound the Baltic States to a co-ordinated action; subsequently, the programme received a joint response from the Baltic side in the form of a common statement issued by the three presidents on 11 January 1994 in support of PfP as a concrete means for working out co-operations between NATO and the Baltic countries.

Shortly thereafter, the PfP-framework document was signed by each of the countries: Lithuania on 27 January, Estonia on 2 February and Latvia on 14 February. Their wish to join NATO was also confirmed in a joint communiqué of the three foreign ministers on 15 February 1994. The need to implement PfP tasks necessitated common Baltic military activities such as the joint air surveillance and monitoring system, a common mine-sweeper squadron and the Baltic Battalion. The creation of the latter in September 1994 has been the most tangible expression of Baltic unity in terms of a collective regional thinking and acting on international security measures. This undertaking became successful largely with the assistance of the "external component" i.e., support and guidance from Britain and the Scandinavian countries.

The race for NATO membership was further heated up by the publication, "Study on NATO Enlargement" from September 1995, as well as from follow-up consultations between the Atlantic Alliance and aspiring members. As prescribed in the relevant study, the enlargement of common defence benefits for the new members contributed extensively to a political rhetoric within the Baltics entirely bound to the notion of emphasising NATO-membership as the ultimate option for each state.[18] The statement by the Latvian Foreign Ministry spokesman that "Latvia does not see any alternative to full-fledged membership in NATO"[19] became the shared and predominant future vision of the other two Baltic States.

Consequently, the Baltic States have offered a co-ordinated and common response in the form of certain larger frameworks which primarily address the very concrete political security proposals of the West. PfP serves as the most distinct example in this sense. In addition, political declarations and statements referring to the evolutionary process of NATO have provided the Baltic States with heightened expectations as to the possibility of obtaining security guarantees from the Atlantic Alliance. However, the main "hard" security objective – NATO membership – has indeed also contributed to the discourse regarding the extent and character of a subregional Baltic military co-operation as the concrete inter-Baltic strategy to strengthen security.

Nato: determining the inter-Baltic military co-operation

As a subject for political discussions, inter-Baltic military co-operation has been an important security political issue of the Baltic States throughout the period of regained independence, not so much for the necessity of such a co-operation but rather for its potentiality and prospects. Among Baltic politicians and military elite there still exists controversial views as to how best estimate this form of co-operation. Politicians with executive power primarily evaluate it as a questionable experiment lacking in any solid grounds given the Baltic countries' limited resources; consequently, it remains on the level of ad hoc activities. Their counterparts, mostly from among the legislative authorities as well as various independent observers, insist that the formation of the military-political alliance between the Baltic States is a very concrete foreign policy line and, hence, needs considerably more attention.

Since 1994 the inter-Baltic legislative body, the Baltic Assembly, has signed three main resolutions concerning the common defence dimension of the three states. Subsequently, on 13 November 1994 the Baltic Assembly adopted the resolution concerning military co-operation between the Baltic States. It was emphasised that the tasks arising from participation in the European collective security system could be fulfilled "only by defence co-operation and a mutual assistance agreement which would provide the legal bases for co-operation between the Baltic States in the spheres of defence and national security".[20]

The idea of mutual military assistance was further stressed by the 7th session of the Baltic Assembly in December 1995 in Tallinn. The Baltic Assembly resolution, adopted on 2 December 1995, declared that "a threat posed to one of the three states shall be regarded as a threat to all three".[21] However, since no defence agreement between the three states had been completed within the period of thirteen months, there was nothing to do but repeat this need.

The third attempt to urge the Estonian, Latvian and Lithuanian governments to jointly bring the countries' militaries up to NATO standards was made at the 9th Session of the Baltic Assembly on 5–6 October, 1996 in Riga. It was US Secretary of Defence William Perry's 27 September 1996 announcement at the NATO Summit in Bergen that the Baltics would not be included in the first wave of NATO expansion which served as the impetus to again argue over the common Baltic defence structure. The outcome of discussions by Baltic politicians was most transparently articulated by a Lithuanian representative saying that, "The answer is not alliance, but co-operation".[22]

According to the evaluation of some Baltic politicians, the reason why the common political level has not gone much beyond the verbal means is largely due to the advisory mandate of a Baltic Assembly which holds no influence over the state budgets and thus remains "a well-meaning talk shop".[23] In fact, the primary reason why the idea of creating a common defence union, Baltic Military Union or Baltic Military Pact is continuously considered off the agenda is because of the very distinct gap between the political will and military capabilities of the three states.

However, the controversy surrounding this subject has also to do with the specific way in which the Baltics reason with the entity of a common military. The initial counter-arguments to a Baltic Military Alliance – deduced from historical failure[24] – have been complemented by additional statements which refer to the strategy of NATO membership. The arguments against the creation of the Baltic Military Pact (or Baltic Military Alliance) may be grouped into seven categories summarised as follows:

1 The creation of a Baltic States Military Alliance would be in contradiction with their main goal – membership in NATO – because NATO does not admit new members as blocks. Thus, the Baltic Military Union would best serve the interests of those who aim to exclude Latvia, Lithuania and Estonia from NATO;

2 The Baltic States should not conduct any policy that might allow the international community to perceive them as different from the Eastern and Central European Countries who do not aim at establishing "mini-alliances";

3 The Baltic Military Alliance could become an obstacle for any of the members of such an alliance should they qualify for early NATO admission;

4 NATO does not have legal responsibilities to provide security guarantees, yet it has the military might as well as the character to defend democratic values. As such, NATO "radiates" security; conversely, Russia "radiates" insecurity – especially towards its neighbouring areas. Aspiring for security, the Balts are thus predetermined to strive for inclusion into NATO;

5 In the event of aggression against any members of the alliance, the Baltic Military Alliance would presuppose legal obligations in assisting its co-allies. However, the Baltic Alliance would lack the necessary military means to encounter any such aggression;

6 The Baltic Military Alliance would be feasible only in the event that its sole existence excluded any aggression towards the three Baltic States. However, this would be beyond its capability for the foreseeable future;

7 The inter-war period evidenced Russia's reaction to attempts at creating the Baltic Military Alliance: either Russia actively intervened in the process (calling it an anti-Russian military block), or insisted on including itself in such a Baltic Alliance.

All these arguments are explanatory by nature and thus reveal that among Baltic politicians, NATO is viewed more as an organisation of military than political nature. Consequently, this point of departure indicates to the Balts that in order to become a full member of the Atlantic Alliance, "the military capability must be increased"[25]. Within this context, the inter-Baltic defence alignment is not estimated to provide the allies with considerable and credible increase of their potential.

The counter-arguments of those *favouring* the creation of the Baltic Military Alliance can be generalised as follows:

1 Since NATO has no legal responsibilities to provide the Balts with security guarantees, Baltic security problems should not be mixed with NATO's. Hence, through joint efforts and by preserving the limited resources of the individual states, the Baltic Military Alliance would be a rather effective means to acquire NATO-required standards;

2 The Baltic Military alliance would demonstrate to the world community the will of the Baltic nations to defend themselves commonly. In turn, this could effectively make them partners rather than beggars vis-à-vis NATO ;

3 Strategically, since any of the Baltic States' early admittance into NATO separately from the others is an impossible scenario, the Baltic Military Alliance would serve as a concrete means to overcome the dangers derived from the security vacuum that would exist prior to their entry;

4 The sub-regional Baltic Military Alliance should be viewed from the perspective of whether it increases or decreases the general level of stability in the broader regional and continental context;

5 The contemporary Baltic Military Alliance should not be identified with the Baltic Entente of 1934, which prescribed extremely defined activity clauses for all sides. The "new" Alliance must be based on the general principle of 'shared military obligations and responsibilities'.

The arguments supporting the foundation of the Baltic Military Alliance are all bound around the common central idea of 'regionalism'. Given the possible scenarios for NATO enlargement – with the Baltic States not being included in the first (if any) wave of enlargement – these views are most likely to gain support among a wider range of Balts. Siding with the idea of the sub-regional Alliance would not necessarily mean a decrease in the positive image of NATO among the Baltic general public because NATO is (and will continue to be) associated with the primary means of acquiring high-level military standards in the build-up of each country's self-defence system.

The policy of NATO enlargement has not only prompted debates about the potentials and vulnerabilities of the sub-regional Baltic Military Alliance, but it has also triggered concrete NATO proposals on the part of the Baltic States. These September 1996 propositions concern practical steps to strengthen the ties between the Atlantic Alliance and prospective states that have expressed their willingness to join NATO. In Estonia's case, the so-called 'non-paper' is entitled, "Partnership for Security"; the corresponding Lithuanian proposal is called "The Atlantic Partnership". Regardless of the name, they both depart from the common position that 'would-be' NATO members require expanded and intensified activities reaching beyond the present PfP programme. In addition, these countries request that NATO make a distinction between the states who participate in the PfP programme and have expressed their wish to join NATO (Albania, Bulgaria, the Czech Republic, Estonia, Hungary, Latvia, Lithuania, Poland, Romania, Slovakia, Slovenia), and those who take part in PfP yet do not aspire to the Atlantic Alliance (Russia, the Ukraine and supposedly Finland).

The Estonian version of the proposal primarily centres on the implementation of practical activities as well as on the role of NATO regional headquarters. It stresses the need for the PfP countries to establish NATO legations and military missions as well as emphasises the active inclusion of planning activities and missions in the Combined Joint Task Force headquarters. Under the auspices of the PfP, the Lithuanian plan proposes a special status for countries of the Atlantic Partnership as an obligatory stage to be passed by all partners who eventually become members of the Atlantic Alliance. Compared to the Estonian version, the Lithuanian project appears more ambitious because it also suggests the participation of the Atlantic Partnership countries in major military exercises of the Alliance, including article five missions.

Consequently, one might argue that through its pure existence as the main and most convincing international defence organisation, NATO has shaped the security and defence policies of all three Baltic States. In the same regard, the Atlantic Alliance has also contributed explicitly to the establishment of a Baltic defence sector which has basically had to start from scratch. Additionally, it has served to pull the Balts towards tenser military co-operation within the Partnership for Peace programme. Finally, it has been an important 'striving force' for the Balts to begin thinking in terms of their own part in the regional and continental security arrangements of the future. However, the Atlantic Alliance's eastward enlargement policy, in conjunction with the Baltics' concern of becoming excluded from this process for the foreseeable future, has caused these states not to link up too closely in the hope they may increase their individual chances of accession.

EU membership: the common political-security perspective of the Baltic States

The other perspective goal of the Baltic States – full membership in the European Union – is estimated by all three countries to be a crucial means in tying Estonia, Latvia and Lithuania economically and politically to Europe. Membership in the EU is equated with a consolidation of democratic achievements, increased economic and social welfare, and stabilised relations with neighbours i.e., a strengthening of the three Baltic States' capabilities. To Baltic authorities, recent past activities such as the Free Trade Agreements between each of the Baltic States and the EU beginning in 1995, participation in the European Stability Pact since the spring of 1995, individual Association Agreements from the summer of 1995, along with the handing in of official applications for EU membership at the end of 1995 indicate both the rapid advancement towards the Union as well as the realistic prospect of joining it in the not-too-distant future.

Since 1995 the Baltic States have also created certain individual institutional instruments in preparation for membership in the EU: the European Affairs Minister in the government as well as the European Integration Bureau under the minister's jurisdiction, and a prime minister-led European Integration Council responsible for co-ordinating upcoming integration issues in the government. These institutions for facilitating the Baltic-EU integration policy exist in Estonia and Latvia, and have corresponding structures in Lithuania as well. The Baltic countries regard the EU as a very concrete political security dimension of their states. According to opinion polls, the positive image of the EU in Estonia, Latvia and Lithuania is strongly associated with the belief that "the EU helps to maintain peace in Europe".[26]

It is through an EU framework that the security theory of Barry Buzan – addressing the broader scope of security forms over military forms and its explicitly growing impact on the post-Cold War international community[27] – also becomes evident to the Baltic States. As an example, the EU is perceived as a concrete means of projecting stability and security for the young democracies of the Baltics. However, it should be noted that the Baltic States are still at an early stage of creating the necessary broader and tighter contacts with the Union.

These bases include, first and foremost, the 'harmonisation of the legislation'. With a total of 1,300 EU directives solely for the level known as 'Stage One' in the EU White Paper, they include fundamental regulations for the single market and its governmental institutions which, in case of the Baltic States, are still in the process of adapting to democratic requirements. In addition, their economic differences within the Baltic context are remarkable. Comparative opinion polls indicate that 57 per cent of Estonians are satisfied with the way things are going and the direction the country is following. In Latvia, the number is 35 per cent whereas in Lithuania, 30 per cent are of a positive opinion.[28]

The differences largely derive from the economic conditions experienced at the general public level. Given the differences in the speed by which economic reforms are carried out in the three Baltic States, as well as by an EU largely associated with economic prosperity, it is thus possible to explain Lithuania's high percentage of those favouring immediate EU membership and Estonia's more modest level. According to data presented by the Central and Eastern Eurobarometer's 1996 survey, 86 per cent of Lithuanians claiming the right to vote on Lithuanian matters would vote 'FOR' joining the European Union "in the event there were a referendum on the question of EU membership tomorrow". In Latvia the percentage would be 80 and in Estonia 76.[29] Thus, it is not surprising that the drive towards EU membership is marked by obvious competition between Estonia, Latvia and Lithuania.

In this context, the slight differences in timing with respect to the signing of agreements and the handing in of applications are of minor importance. However, these time differences are often exploited by certain Baltic politicians as arguments to prove the speedier and, therefore, more advanced EU policy of one particular Baltic State over another. The competitiveness is most notable on the level of political rhetoric where Baltic co-operation vis-à-vis the EU remains much too general in verbal terms. "It has become a custom among the politicians of the Baltic States to surprise each other with declarations and statements made separately in the direction of Western countries".[30]

Within the sphere of economics, Estonia has been most vocal in promoting its successful reform policy. Estonia was also the only one to sign both the Free Trade Agreement and the Association Agreement with the EU – without a transition period. Several Western analysts have also pointed out Estonia as being economically and politically ahead of the other two Baltic States.[31] However, the unsettled border agreement with Russia along with their complex minority problems provide for solid counter-arguments to their being in better position vis-à-vis the other two Baltic countries with respect to the EU.

To balance its economic drawbacks, Lithuania has chosen to concentrate on constructive and business-like relations with Russia in addition to managing its minority issues internally.[32] It can be further argued that in actively aspiring to CEFTA membership, Lithuania is striving to facilitate a supposedly more effective Westward integration entity than provided through the Baltic co-operation. As stated by a Lithuanian foreign ministry official, "membership in CEFTA is evaluated as going in the same direction as entering the European Union".[33] Lithuania's frequent references to the Baltics as an entity with purely geographic meaning, along with references to how it and Poland belong to the same geo-political area, suggests that Lithuania considers it politically necessary to detach itself from Estonia and Latvia while linking up with Poland, the most likely candidate for both the EU and NATO.

However, in striving towards membership in the European Union, competition has been co-ordinated with efforts for greater economic co-operation among the Balts. The year 1996 is reasonably rich in these intentions. In the summer of 1996, the Free Trade Agreement merged the Baltic markets in the area of manufactured and agricultural goods by removing tariffs and quotas on inter-Baltic trade. Since the autumn of 1996, the creation of a joint customs union among the three states has been addressed as an important criterion in determining the economic role of the Baltics in a broader international context.[34]

Baltic authorities have acknowledged that "co-operation must be developed in this area in order to allow for integration into the European Union".[35] For the customs union to become a reality, several areas such as transit, customs system, trade legislation and statistics systems need to be co-ordinated; correspondingly, respective agreements must be worked out as well. The idea of a common economic Baltic area has also been duly recognised by the three presidents in their November 1996 meeting at Riga.[36] Consequently, in terms of pursuing an EU policy, the role as an economic "bridge" would, at the very least, obtain a more positive connotation for the Balts.

Conclusion

The Baltic countries entered into a period of state-building process in the midst of the most profound changes in the international environment since the end of the Cold War. The mixed influence of historical memories, Soviet legacies and Baltic interpretations of the dynamic processes of Euro-integration have been the primary determinants in the way the re-established states position and see themselves. Subsequently, the primary international organisations shaping the contemporary Western world – NATO and the EU – have played the major role in contributing to the state-building process of all three Baltic countries.

First and foremost, since membership in these organisations is the officially declared political priority of all three, Estonia, Latvia and Lithuania have been forced to distinguish and acknowledge the main obstacles for achieving this goal. Furthermore, in terms of Estonian-Russian border problems, Latvian minority issues and Lithuanian economic matters, it has driven each to work with these problems and implement the necessary mechanisms to deal with the adversities. Successful solutions are neither quick nor easy to reach, yet it is essential to be able to recognise individual problems and rank them in a broader context to the particular interests of each individual country. Thus, the pre-accession EU questionnaires on domestic and foreign policy areas have helped to identify the most problematic areas for the governments of these states.

In Estonia's case, it has revealed that its local industry development is beyond the level of Albania's and is comparable to that of Romania and Bulgaria; tourism and services are its strengths.[37] In the case of Latvia, according to the Latvian Minister for European Union Affairs Aleksander Kristeins "the obvious need for new taxation and customs codes has become explicit".[38]

Within these processes, the overall international condition and development of the Baltic States suggests that for the foreseeable future, security will consist of mixed forms and combinations of international co-operation in order to guarantee stability. The different international models and forms of activities connected with "hard" security are by nature already determined to increase military co-operation among Estonia, Latvia and Lithuania. PfP, by way of its enhancing the operational aspect in the more routine involvement of Baltic partner countries in decision-making and planning activities as well as with the use of political consultations for the regional dimension, is the most obvious and concrete project providing for deeper multilateral and integrated security co-operation. Clearly, this is the area where the Balts are indeed continuing to be most co-operative since, as the Estonian Minister of Defence has expressed, "here we are not competitors, as it may seem in some areas of economy, but rather partners vitally interested in each other".[39]

This new framework of international security co-operation activities departs from the positive scenarios based upon the assumption that "Russia will also remain linked to democracy in the future".[40] In this context, Russia is seen from the Western point of view both from the standpoint of NATO, as well as from the EU, as an active participant in these new forms of regional co-operation. The processes of European integration and the development of a European security system all maintain that the Baltics remain indistinguishable from the Russian dimension as countries dependent on the Russian political scene. Thus, as pointed out by James Franklin Collin, US Ambassador-at-large for the Newly Independent States, "the development of peaceful and normal relations between the Balts and their neighbours, including Russia, are very much in American interests".[41]

Unmistakably, the Baltic States will not be able to escape this reality when aspiring for a credible security identity. Given the geo-political realities, and considering the long-term perspectives of international relations, the three Baltic countries could obviously increase their international credibility by striving for a common security identity rather than focusing on differences and advocating individuality. Constructive co-operation is, therefore, the means available to be used more profoundly.

With 'regionalism' being a key-word in contemporary World politics, it is indeed the *regional entity* of the three Baltic States which can perform a much more concrete European as well as global role than what could be available to each country separately.

Notes

1 In Estonia the Popular Front was founded in April 1988; in Latvia and Lithuania the corresponding organisations were established in October 1988.

2 The law on the Estonian,Latvian and Lithuanian transition to economic independence starting from March 1990 was finally passed by the Congress of the Peoples' Deputies of the USSR on 27 July 1989.

3 See: Declaration of Concord and Co-operation by the Republic of Estonia, Republic of Latvia and Republic of Lithuania from 12 May 1990. In: Restoration of the Independence of the Republic of Estonia. Selection of Legal Acts (1988–1991), Advig Kiris (ed.), Ministry of Foreign Affairs of the Republic of Estonia, Tallinn, 1991.

4 For studies on the issues of ethnopolicy see, i.e., research works carried out by the ethnopolicy working group of the Institute of International and Social Studies, Estonia, in the period 1992–1996.

5 For more elaborate discussions on the Baltic States and neutrality see ,for example, Andris Ozolinsh, *The Policies of the Baltic Countries vis-a- vis the CSCE, NATO and WEU.* In: The Foreign Policies of the Baltic Countries: Basic Issues, Pertti Joenniemi and Juris Prikulis (eds.), Centre of Baltic-Nordic History and Political Studies, Riga, 1994, pp. 49–74; Mare Haab, *Is Neutrality a Foreign-Policy Option for Small Nation States? The Case of Estonia.* In: New Actors on the International Arena: the Foreign Policy of the Baltic Countries, Pertti Joenniemi and Peeter Vares (eds.), Tampere Peace Research Institute Research Report No. 50, 1993, pp. 73–81.

6 President Yeltsin, Foreign Minister Kozyrev, General Lebed, Mayor of Moscow Juri Luzhkov, to name only some, have threatened to use military means against the Baltic States.From among the recent statements see, i.e.: Russian newspapers *Mezhdunarodnaya Zhizn,* No. 6, October 1995; *Izvestiya* 12 October 1995; Interfax/BNS 7 May 1996.

7 See: *Report On the Security Concept of Russian Federation,* Russian Institute of Strategic Studies, Moscow, 1993, p. 8. An even more direct military threat towards the Baltic States is advocated in the document entitled "The Conceptual Bases of Countermeasures to the External Threat Directed Against the National Security of the Russian Federation", compiled by the Moscow based Institute of Strategic Studies in October 1995. See: Russian daily *Segodnya,* 20 October 1995.

8 Ibid.

9 Ibid.

10 See for example, Latvia: National Security Concept , approved by the Latvian National Security Council on 22 May 1995. In: *The Monthly Survey of the Baltic and Post-Soviet Politics,* February 1996, Tallinn, Panor-Press Sakala Centre, pp. 90–97.

11 See: the interview by Lilian Shevtsova, in: Estonian daily *Eesti Päevaleht,* 4 December 1996.

12 This complex problem needs a separate study, which is beyond the limits of the present paper. Still, it may be argued that the primary reasons for

high priority in military security derive form the leangthy experience under the totalitarian regime as well as the short-term inter-war experience of independent statehood.

13 Lithuania has signed bilateral agreements of co-operation with all its neighbouring countries (with Russia in 1991, with Poland in 1994, with Belarus in 1995 and with Latvia in 1996).

14 In 1989 ethnic Latvians comprised 52 per cent of the total population of Latvia, by 1994 the figure had reached to 54.23. For more detailed data see: Zhaneta Ozolina, Latvian Security Policy. In: The Baltic States Search for Security, Atis Lejinsh and Daina Bleier (eds.), Latvian Institute of International Affairs, Riga, 1996, pp. 23–57.

15 Source: Estonian Statistical Office, 16 October 1996.

16 Estonian daily *Postimess* 27 November 1992.

17 See: NATO Summit Declaration, 10–11 January 1994.

18 See: NATO Study on enlargement, 1995.

19 See: *The Baltic Times,* November 7–13, 1996.

20 See: Baltic Assembly Resolution Concerning Military Co-operation Between the Baltic States. The Baltic Assembly 5th Session, 11–13 November 1994, Vilnius. In: **The Monthly Survey of the Baltic and Post-Soviet Politics**, November 1994, Panor-Press Sakala Centre, Tallinn, p. 38.

21 See: Resolution on the Principles of Unity of the Baltic States, The Baltic Assembly. 7th Session, 1–2 December 1995, Tallinn. In: **The Monthly Survey of the Baltic and Post-Soviet Politics**, December 1995, Tallinn, Panor-Press Sakala Centre, Tallinn, p. 1.

22 These words belong to the Lithuanian Baltic Assembly Presidium member Egidijus Bickauskas. See: *The Baltic Times,* October 10–16, 1996.

23 Ibid.

24 An Estonian-Latvian military union was created in 1923, but Lithuania never joined it. Now Lithuania has again asserted that the creation of a Baltic military union would be non-productive in fulfilling the main aspirations of the states. See, for example, the Baltic weekly, *the Baltic Independence,* January 26 – February 1, 1996; Estonian Daily, *Eesti Sõnumileht,* January 24, 1996.

25 See for example the interview of Siim Kallas, the Estonian Minister of Foreigh Affairs, to the Estonian monthly *Luup,* No. 21, 14 October 1996 p. 16–19.

26 See: Central and Eastern Eurobarometer Survey No. 6, 1996.

27 B.Buzan et al., **The European Security Order Recast, Scenarios for the Post-Cold War Era** (London: Pinter 1990).

28 Ibid.

29 Ibid.

30 See: the Estonian daily *Postimees,* August 18, 1996.

31 For a most interesting and useful study on this subject see, for example, Ronald D. Asmus and Robert C. Nurick, "NATO Enlargement and the Baltic States", in: *Survival,* Vol. 38, No. 2 (Summer 1996).

32 A recent example to this is the speech of the President of Lithuania Algirdas Brazauskas presented to the EU in October 1996. See: the Estonian monthly *Luup,* No. 22 (27), October 28, 1996, p. 33.

33 See: Comments on Lithuania's relations to CEFTA made by the Lithuanian Foreign Ministry Secretary Algimantas Rimkunas in: *The Baltic Times*, September 12–18, 1996.

34 The creation of the Baltic customs union was the main topic also at the regional conference in Tallinn in October 1996. High officials from the three Baltic States and international organisations addressed also the promotion of trade among the three countries and the development of Baltic endeavours in other markets. See,i.e., Estonian Rewiev, Vol. 6 No. 43, October 21–27, 1996.

35 Ibid.

36 See: Estonian daily *Eesti Påevaleht*, 27 November 1996.

37 See the arguments presented by the Estonian European Affairs Minister Endel Lippmaa in : *The Baltic Times*, August 1–7, 1996.

38 Ibid.

39 Similar views have been stated by various Baltic politicians on different occasions. This idea was expressed by the Estonian Minister of Defence Andrus Öövel in his speech at the international conference "Estonia and the European Union" on October 19, 1995 in Tallinn.

40 See, for example , the study by Ronald D. Asmus and F. Stephan Larrabee, NATO and the Have-Nots Reassurance After Enlargement. In: *Foreign Affairs*, Vol. 74, No. 6.

41 See: *The Baltic Times*, August 1–7, 1996.

Chapter 2

The Baltic States and Europe
The Quest for Security

Peter van Ham

Introduction

The European Union (EU) as well as NATO have committed themselves to admit new members in the years to come. Both organizations have yet to specify the "who" and "when"-questions of enlargement, but although early membership of the Baltic states has not been ruled out, a consensus is slowly emerging that these three small states will not be among the first tranche of new members.

This chapter will examine the policies of the EU and NATO *vis-à-vis* the Baltic states, and will also pay attention to the roles of the Western European Union (WEU) and the Organization for Security and Cooperation in Europe (OSCE) in providing some form of security for this region. Underlying the analysis of this chapter are the following questions: (1) how do the Baltic states fit into Europe's evolving security framework? (2) what factors will influence future membership of the Baltic states in the EU/WEU and NATO? And (3) how can the West contribute to consolidating the security of the Baltic states, short of offering them full membership of Europe's key security institutions? Obviously these are difficult questions to answer, not only because Europe's security environment is in a state of drift, but also because the EU, WEU and NATO are themselves in the process of adapting to new post-Cold War roles. This chapter will therefore not attempt to give definite answers, but limit itself to identifying and examining the main security trends with respect to the Baltic region.

The EU: is "non-military" security sufficient?

Perhaps it is now more true than ever that security does not always have to come out of the barrel of a gun. All Central European countries are focussing on developing a stable market economy, meanwhile building a cohesive civil society and a parliamentary democracy. Joining the EU is therefore the top priority on the foreign policy agenda of Central European countries, who realize that although the Union can not provide an Article 5 military security guarantee *à la* NATO and WEU, full EU membership will make them an integral part of the process towards European unity. Finish President Martti Ahtisaari stated in December 1996, that "as a member of the European Union, Finland is part of a community of political solidarity. A threat to one member state is directed against the whole community."[1] Austria's former Minister of Foreign Affairs Alois Mock, has even argued that EU membership in itself would suffice to guarantee his country's security: "The Union's cohesion and solidarity derives from the interdependence and partial fusion of the economies of member states and thus offers to each partner a security guarantee *which might well be more reliable than formal treaty commitments.*"[2] Although this point is not often raised, its validity is undisputable: it is inconceivable that a EU member state which participates fully in the three pillars of the Union would, in the case of external military aggression, even in the absence of official security guarantees, not be assisted by its European partners. In this sense, EU membership may provide a form of "non-military" security based on enhanced political solidarity and a firm basis of economic interdependence.

The EU has initially been reluctant to formulate clear-cut criteria for membership. In most Europe agreements, which the EU has now signed with all ten Central European countries (i.e. Bulgaria, the Czech Republic, Estonia, Hungary, Latvia, Lithuania, Poland, Rumania, Slovenia and Slovakia – Europe agreements with the Baltic states were signed in June 1995), an article is included stipulating the need for respect of democratic principles and human rights as a *sine qua non* for association with the Union. In some of the Europe agreements there are explicit references to the respect of the rule of law and human rights, including minority rights. Furthermore, in most cases, an explicit "emergency clause" makes it possible to suspend the agreement in case of violations of these principles.

Most Central European countries have called for a clear set of criteria as well as a time-frame which could guide their efforts to become eligible for membership. At the Copenhagen summit of the EU in June 1993, it was agreed "that the associated countries in

Central and Eastern Europe that so desire shall become members of the European Union". The EU also formulated the following general conditions for membership:

- stability of institutions guaranteeing democracy, the rule of law, human rights and respect for and protection of minorities;
- capacity to assume the obligations of membership (the so-called *acquis communautaire*);
- capacity to cope with competitive pressures and market forces within the EU;
- endorsement of the objectives of political, economic and monetary union; and
- the EU's capacity to absorb new member states while maintaining the momentum of European integration should not be undermined.

The EU has initially been equally reluctant to specify concretely what level of economic development or political stability is expected from the Central European candidate countries. There is little doubt that the Copenhagen conditions have been kept vague on purpose, and that their assessment will be primarily politically motivated.[3]

The EU's Intergovernmental Conference (IGC), which started in March 1996 and is tasked to review (and change) the Maastricht Treaty on European Union, is preparing the way for the accession of up to ten new member states. It is clear that without institutional reform of the EU – streamlining its decision making process and making room for new members in all its three pillars – enlargement will be seriously delayed.[4] Most EU member states, as well as the European Commission and the European Parliament, agree that institutional reform is a *sine qua non* for widening the Union. Central European countries are not actively involved in the IGC, but they are regularly briefed (at ministerial as well as ambassadorial level) on the development of the IGC. Nevertheless, they all have to wait and hope that the Fifteen will muster the political will to make difficult choices and find a way to square the circle of "widening" and "deepening" simultaneously.

In June 1996, some light was shed on the Union's concrete enlargement plans when the European Commission declared that the earliest probable date for Central European applicant states to join will be around 2002. The Commission argued that enlargement is likely to proceed in phases, taking into account the economic strength and political maturity of the candidate country.[5] This longer-than-expected timetable for membership comes as a disappointment, but nevertheless seems realistic given the complexity of conducting accession negotiations with so many applicants.

The timing of the enlargement negotiations will be important. Germany had put some pressures on its partners to give priority to Poland, the Czech Republic and Hungary, arguing (quite correctly) that these countries are in the forefront of economic and political reform. This suggestion, however, has met with much criticism from both EU member states as well as from most of the other Central European countries. At the EU's Madrid Summit of December 1995, it was therefore agreed that accession negotiations will start with *all* candidate countries *simultaneously*, six months after the conclusion of the IGC. Depending on when the IGC will end, this means that negotiations will probably start in the first months of 1998. Around that time, the Commission will have to present its official Opinion on each individual candidate country's prospects of joining the Union, as well as a composite paper on enlargement which will assess the overall effects of enlargement on the EU's policies, as well as a report on the financial impact of enlargement. These are important documents which will provide an indication of the candidate country's state of reform as well as the state of mind of the EU and its Member States on enlargement. On 26 July 1996, all ten EU associate states handed in an elaborate questionnaire on the basis of which the European Commission will develop its Opinion on the accession of new member states. In the meantime, candidate countries must continue harmonizing their legislation with a total of 1300 EU directives, including 400 that determine the fundamental regulations for the Single Market and the reform of governmental institutions.

Most West European analysts and officials continue to view the Baltic states as a group, as a cohesive region, despite their obvious differences in background and economic and political achievements. But although all three Baltic states will start accession negotiations simultaneously, their different economic and political circumstances may well make it possible that one of them will join the Union somewhat ahead of the others. Estonia does not make a secret of its wish to take a fast-track to the EU, claiming that its superior economic performance makes it eligible to join the post-Maastricht Union. There is little doubt that among the Baltic states, Estonia's economic situation is relatively favorable. Not only has Tallinn managed to avoid the major banking crises that have played havoc with the financial systems of Latvia and Lithuania, it has also managed to sustain real GDP growth for more than two years. After a real GDP growth of 4.7 percent and 3.8 percent in 1994 and 1995 resp., a further growth of 3.5 and 3.3 percent is forecast for 1996 and 1997 resp. For Latvia, these figures are less positive (a real GDP growth of 2.0 percent in 1994, a decline of 2.0 percent in 1995, and a forecast of 0.6 percent and 2.0 percent growth in 1996 and 1997 resp.); for Lithuania the figures show moderate growth (a real GDP growth of 1.0 percent and 3.5 percent in 1994 and 1995 resp., and a forecast of 2.0 percent growth for 1997.)[6] Estonia also has the lowest unemployment rate in the region, although it suffers from somewhat higher inflation than its Baltic neighbors. It is also important to point out that Estonia has established a trade regime which is among the most liberal in the whole of Central and Eastern Europe. Although Tallinn still has some way to go to adjust to the EU's *acquis communautaire*, it definitely is the frontrunner of the three Baltic states in relations with the Union. Estonia applied for EU membership in November 1995 (Latvia applied in October 1995; Lithuania in December 1995). The EU signed a Free Trade Agreement with Estonia in July 1994 (as well as with Lithuania and Latvia), which went into force in January 1995.

But it is, of course, not only economic criteria that will have to be taken into account; political and geo-strategic consideration will also weigh heavy on the minds of West European policy makers.[7] The protracted border problems between Tallinn and Moscow are considered a serious obstacle to early Estonian EU membership. The political question of whether the Tartu Peace Treaty (of 1920) is still in force or not, remains a point of contention in Estonia's relations with Russia.[8] President Lennart Meri has referred to the Treaty as "Estonia's birth certificate", which serves to indicate that the Estonian state was born in 1918, and not in 1991. Time and again, EU officials have stressed that stable borders are a prerequisite for enlargement, which would be especially important in the Estonian case since its borders with Russia will most likely also become the outer limit of the EU. In this context Estonia's minister responsible for European Affairs indicated: "It is serious. The Russian Federation does not even have a treaty with Japan [on fixing borders], and it is not ready for a treaty with us, which is destabilizing for the whole region."[9] What is more, Estonia's 80,000 Russian citizens are far from integrated in society, and voted predominantly for the Communist candidate in the July 1996 Russian presidential elections (77 percent of the votes cast). The last thing the EU wants to add to its problems are new member states who still have unresolved minority issues, especially when they are minorities who have Russia as their "motherland".

EU membership is also at the top of the foreign policy agenda of Lithuania and Latvia. Both countries are likely to find different obstacles on their way towards EU membership: Lithuania with its proximity to the highly militarized Russian enclave of Kaliningrad, and Latvia with its large Russian minority. As indicated earlier, both countries have also managed their economic reform programmes less successfully than Estonia. It therefore came as no surprise that the first EU/Latvian working group, meeting in March 1996, concluded that Riga still had significant work to do to adjust its legislation to EU standards. The EU also suggested that Latvian officials charged with the country's integration into the Union should better coordinate their work. But Brussels has, of course, not limited itself to criticism; through its PHARE-programme, the Union is actively engaged in supporting the goals of accession of all three Baltic states. For example, for the period 1996–2000 the EU will spend US$ 187 m. on education exchange programmes, training, infrastructure development as well as programmes aimed at the approximation of Lithuanian laws and standards to the Union's *acquis*. Similar assistance programmes have been devised for Latvia and Estonia. In July 1995, the EU has also approved special European Integration PHARE programmes for the Baltic states which are specifically focussed on preparing these countries for accession.

It is clear that Scandinavian support for the Baltic states will be crucial for early entry into the EU. Scandinavian countries not only continue to make the case for the Baltic states in Brussels (in the EU, WEU as well as NATO), but are also in the forefront to assist the Baltic states in strengthening their defense capabilities in a wide variety of practical ways.[10] For example, all Scandinavian countries assist the Baltic Battalion (Baltbat – which is coordinated by Denmark and trains in Latvia)[11], and offer training for future Baltic officers at their Military Academies. Sweden has also indicated that it wants to set up a specific regional PfP-training center on the island of Gotland, where the Baltic states will receive preparatory training in order to better participate in international joint exercises.[12] Sweden has initially emphasized so-called low-profile "sovereignty support" to the Baltic states, including coastguard and frontier guard assistance. Direct military assistance has been kept limited in order not to give Russia reasons to protest against the military rearmament of the Baltic states. But this now seems to have changed, since Stockholm has promised (in Autumn 1996) to donate some fully functioning war vessels (which will become redundant after the reform of the Swedish Defence Forces), as well as other surplus military materiel to the Baltic states.[13] Swedish Defence Forces are now already helping the Baltic states to build up a joint naval force whose primary task is to take care of the mine clearing along the Baltic sea coast. The idea is that in the future, mine clearing will be part of the Baltic states' contribution to PfP exercises. (This joint Baltic naval force – provisionally called Baltron – has been labeled a "Baltbat at sea.") Most Scandinavian countries also provide support to the Baltic sea and air border protection system (although the latter is still only at the design stage).[14] As another example of Nordic solidarity one could mention the assistance agreement between Latvia and Denmark designed to help Riga prepare for EU membership, as well as the symbolically important first foreign trip of Sweden's Prime Minister Göran Persson to Estonia (in April 1996).

Despite the obvious need for collective action, effective Baltic cooperation to join Europe's security institutions still remains the exception rather than the rule. Baltic heads of states do frequently meet in summits (a Baltic Council of Ministers was set up in June 1994), reiterating their shared commitment to join Europe. In the Vilnius summit of late-May 1996, the three Baltic leaders adopted a "Joint Declaration of the Baltic Presidents on Partnership for Integration", which stresses the common will to integrate their countries in the EU and NATO, and calls for a simultaneous start of the EU and NATO accession process with all three Baltic states. The Joint Declaration concludes with the plea: "Because of our joint commitment to these goals, no one should try to play one of our countries off against another. As we were when we strove to recover our independence, so, too, now we are united and will remain so."[15] The Declaration also stresses that the Baltic desire to join the EU and NATO is to be part of a united Europe, rather than a "fear of a third country". A few months later, the three Baltic Presidents declared that "Vague promises for the Baltic states to integrate into the Alliance might destabilise the Baltic security space."[16] Given the fact that Baltic cooperation offers much room for improvement, the decision to set up a (modest) Secretariat of the Baltic Council of Ministers in Tallinn is a step in the right direction.[17] The formation of a joint Baltic working group to coordinate arms systems standardization efforts (an important element to prepare for NATO membership) should also be applauded.[18]

Behind the façade of these regular "Joint Declarations", each Baltic state continues to use its bilateral ties to increase its accession chances. This is, of course, only to be expected, but it does also detract somewhat from the effectiveness of the process of political cooperation among the Baltic states. The remark by Estonian Prime Minister Lennart Meri (during his visit to Brussels in late-March 1996), that EU enlargement should take place on a case-by-case basis without considering the Baltic states as a separate group, has met with strong criticism in Riga and Vilnius. Mr Meri argued that the "group of countries"-approach may have its merits in fields like defense and security, but that it has no similar justification in the economic area.[19] Estonia also makes the best of its close historical ties with Finland to further its cause. Lithuania and Latvia are, of course, also making the most of their comparative advantages. For example, Lithuania makes active use of its close (albeit at times problematic) historical ties with Poland to improve its relations with the EU. In May 1996, both countries presented a joint document to the EU concerning the intensification of the political dialogue between the Union and its associates. Warsaw and Vilnius also cooperate to establish a combined peacekeeping unit and an airspace management regime.

The Baltic states have also faced a number of disagreements among themselves concerning disputed territory in the Baltic Sea. Latvia and Estonia have quarreled over the waters around the Estonian island of Ruhnu, both countries claiming fishing rights in this part of the Baltic Sea. Latvia and Lithuania have disputed over oil reserves in the Baltic Sea, but this now seems to have been solved. Industrial and agricultural free trade agreements between the Baltic states are already in place, but much remains to be done to improve custom procedures at the borders and intra-Baltic trade is far from optimal.

One of the most important contributions all three Baltic states could make to bring EU, WEU as well as NATO membership closer, is to improve their relations with Russia. Economically, the Baltic states remain highly dependent on trade with Russia and for Lithuania and Latvia, Russia remains the single largest trading partner; for Estonia, trade with Russia comes second only after Finland, even though the Baltic states continue to do their utmost to diversify their trade away from the CIS-area. For Latvia, for example, the EU accounted for 44.1 percent of all export and almost half of all imports, while the share of the CIS fell to 38.3 percent for export in 1995 (in 1994: 42.7 percent), and 28.2 percent for imports (1994: 30.4 percent).

Politically, the most sensitive issues are citizenship and the treatment of Russian minorities. The Baltic states have participated in the EU-sponsored European Stability Pact (within the so-called Baltic Regional Table), in an effort to find a solution for the region's minority and border questions. The OSCE is now involved in monitoring some of the agreements which have resulted from the Stability Pact (see section 4 of this paper). But although improving political relations with Russia is of course a two-way street, West European observers are at times baffled by the seemingly unreasonable positions or provocative approach of some Baltic states towards Moscow. This has led the Russian Duma to call upon President Yeltsin to impose economic sanctions on Estonia, mainly for its alleged mistreatment of ethnic Russians, but also for the solidarity that Estonian MP's expressed for the Chechen rebel fighters.

Russian officials have their own explanation of Estonia's "provocative" attitude towards Moscow, namely that Tallinn is trying to facilitate its integration into Western institutions by invoking "a mythical Russian threat".[20] Although this might be an exaggeration too, there are also Western analysts who argue that "Some Baltic leaders have a more sophisticated but even more dangerous approach. They think that to 'cure' Russia of neo-imperialism (. . .), it needs to suffer another shattering geopolitical defeat, and that NATO expansion up to Russia's borders would provide such a defeat."[21] If this would even be partly true, this would certainly be a counterproductive approach to integrating the Baltic states in the Europe's security framework.

Given the "non-military" security provided by EU membership (or even a closer institutionalized relationship with the Union), the Baltic states might want to consider giving the EU priority over NATO. Until now, Russia has not raised any serious objections to future Baltic EU membership. This can be partly explained by Russia's perception of the EU as principally an economic/trade organization, without a security/defence component. The EU is also not burdened by the stigma of being a Cold War-organization, like NATO.[22] Most analysts in Moscow still fail to see the link established in Maastricht between EU and WEU membership.[23] When WEU offered Associate Partnership-status to nine Central European countries (including the Baltic states) in June 1994, Moscow hardly reacted. It should, however, be recalled that WEU's Article 5 provides a similar security guarantee as the Alliance's Washington Treaty. The fact that all three Baltic states now attend the WEU Permanent Council on a bi-weekly basis and participate regularly in other WEU working groups, indicates that they are considered an integral part of "Central Europe", and therefore potential candidate countries for Europe's security institutions.

It is interesting to see that Moscow occasionally even suggests WEU membership as a possible alternative to NATO enlargement.[24] This idea has found little support in Western Europe.[25] Not only would it undermine the current objective of making EU, WEU and NATO enlargement broadly congruous, but the functional relationship between WEU and NATO would also be impeded were membership of those two organizations to diverge (currently all full members of WEU are also NATO Allies). Probably for this reason, NATO has clearly stated that it favors the "eventual broad congruence of European membership in NATO, EU and WEU", and that it would "give particular consideration to countries with a perspective of EU membership" when the time comes to decide on the "who" – question of NATO enlargement.[26]

The IGC will most likely find a way to link the EU and WEU closer together. WEU has already prepared a detailed analysis of the possible options (in November 1995).[27] One of the options calls for an arrangement to provide for participation by all EU member states in joint peacekeeping and crisis management operations which would then be conducted by WEU. This option is now supported by most EU member states (and has been the main topic of a joint memorandum issued by Finland and Sweden on 25 April 1996)[28], with the notable exception of the United Kingdom and Denmark. This would not amount to a merger of the EU and WEU (an idea which has little support among the Fifteen) but WEU's collective defence commitments would be placed outside the new EU-framework; no country would be compelled to join the "defence annex", or "collective defence protocol" to the new EU Treaty which would be open to all EU member states. It would, however, go without saying that *all* current WEU full members would also subscribe to the new EU "defence protocol". Such an outcome of the IGC would certainly be interesting for the Baltic states, since they could then possibly join Sweden, Finland and Austria as full EU member states, feeling themselves secure *without* an official military security guarantee. For Western Europe and the US, such an option would be preferred over full Baltic WEU and/or NATO membership; it would also have the considerable added benefit of not antagonizing Russia.

Unfortunately, since the reform of the EU and the strengthening of WEU takes more time than anticipated, all Central European countries – including the Baltic states – will have to bide their time. This will be difficult, especially since most Baltic officials fail to see greater problems to joining the EU than those that were satisfactorily solved by Greece, Spain and Portugal. This, however, overlooks the major changes that have taken place since the end of the Cold War. Especially the EU has had to add further "entry criteria" for new members, since the economic and political threshold to membership has increased markedly with the Union's efforts of establishing an Economic and Monetary Union (EMU) and a Common Foreign and Security Policy (CFSP). In the meantime, the Baltic strategic elite should call for more patience; this is especially important since support for the EU in the Baltic states seems to be slowly waning. In 1991, 50 percent of Lithuanians, 45 percent of Latvians and 38 percent of Estonians still had a positive image of the Union; five years later these figures had dropped significantly to 23 percent, 35 and 30 percent resp.[29]

NATO: The Baltic quest for "hard security"

The Baltic states clearly regard NATO as the only organization that can provide them with a "hard" security guarantee. At the same time, most Baltic officials acknowledge that NATO faces serious difficulties in including the Baltic states in the first round of enlargement. Until the "who" and "when"-questions are answered, NATO argues that all countries participating in the dialogue are, in principle, eligible; no country is *a fortiori* ruled in or ruled out. NATO officials also point out that an active participation in the Partnership for Peace (PfP) programme will, for the time being, be the closest thing to a real "security guarantee" that the Baltic states can get.

All Baltic states are trying to substantiate their membership credentials by participating as fully as possible within the PfP, trying to demonstrate that they are not only "consumers" of security, but are, and will be, a valuable asset for the Alliance as a whole. Baltic participation in the Bosnia Implementation Force (IFOR), was therefore symbolically very important. In Bosnia, Baltic forces work together with Swedish, Finnish and Polish contingents in a Nordic Brigade, operating side by side with Russian troops, all under US command and under NATO auspices.

The Baltic states also often participate in PfP military exercises. The *Baltic Challenge '96* exercises held in Latvia in July 1996 in the context of NATO's PfP programme, have been important to train

Baltic troops for future peacekeeping duties. Almost 600 US troops participated in this exercise; a *Baltic Challenge '97* is being planned. The Baltic states also participated in the PfP exercise *Baltic Circle '96*, which took place in Denmark in September-October 1996. Latvia is now considering sending a peacekeeping mission with the UN to Macedonia during 1996, and Estonian troops might well join the UN peacekeeping mission in Lebanon. All three Baltic states also participate in the PfP Planning and Review Process (PARP), which is designed to advance interoperability and increase transparency among Allies and partner countries.

The desire to strengthen ties with NATO in order to ultimately join the Alliance, has already positively influenced cooperation among the Baltic states in the security and defense field (e.g. Baltbat), and has also speeded up internal defence policy reviews. (In Estonia, for example, a new defense policy was finally approved (in April 1996) to intensify Tallinn's bid for early NATO membership.) Recent plans to establish a joint Baltic Sea countries navy squadron should be seen in this context (*supra*). In the meantime, the lack of financial resources continues to be a serious problem for the Baltic states in their efforts to upgrade their armed forces to a level adequate to fully participate in NATO's PfP programme. For example, Estonia's Defense Ministry complained in June 1996 that its defense forces were understaffed by as much as 50 percent, even though the Government had decided in April of that year to double the defense budget from 5 to 10 percent of the state budget for 1997.[30] Apart from spending this money on equipment, infrastructure and salaries, Estonia needs to make its forces NATO-compatible by complying to a number of interoperability objectives (e.g. radio communication frequencies, standardization of fuels for land and maritime forces, English-language capability and common grids and symbols for maps). Obviously, Lithuanian and Latvian forces face similar challenges.

All Baltic states share the concern that they will be left out on their own after a EU, WEU and NATO enlargement which would exclude them. As Lithuania's deputy foreign minister Albinas Januska stated in May 1996: "It is a unique chance in our history to become part of Europe. But we fear that the West might sell us out again."[31] For several reasons, Western analysts and policy makers are concerned that instability in the Baltic region might derail the NATO enlargement process itself. It certainly will be difficult for NATO to combine enlargement with its goal to enhance security in the *whole* of Europe and not contribute to new dividing lines.

In a recent publication, two senior analysts at RAND have made a strong case for NATO (as well as the EU) to develop an enlargement strategy specifically aimed at sustaining Baltic independence and security.[32] They acknowledge that the Baltic states are unlikely to be admitted in the first tranche of new EU and NATO members, given the lack of active and strong support among Europe's key actors as well as in North America. They identify five reasons for this limited support: (1) the Baltic states are not considered of vital strategic interest to Europe's security and stability as a whole; (2) Russia's sensitivities to possible Baltic NATO membership are greater than to other Central European countries; (3) the Alliance is reluctant to take in new members with unresolved minority and border problems; (4) the Baltic states will be difficult to defend; and (5) Kaliningrad would become a thorn in the side of NATO were the Alliance to take in the Baltic states.

The key policy advice of the two RAND analysts (apart from encouraging political and economic reform, as well as Baltic defense cooperation and Nordic-Baltic cooperation), is that the EU should seriously consider including Estonia in the first wave of enlargement. The RAND paper suggests that it should be made clear beforehand to Tallinn that this would – exceptionally – not result in an invitation to also join WEU as a full member, since this would mean a backdoor NATO security guarantee. At the same time they call for an expanded PfP-programme in the Baltic region. The principal benefit from such a strategy would be that it would provide an "institutional manifestation of the West's commitments to and engagement in the Baltic region."

The RAND analysis and recommendations have certainly boosted the debate on the Baltic states and their place in Europe's evolving security framework. Especially (temporarily) de-coupling the semi-automatic link between EU and WEU membership might be a useful, pragmatic solution to the challenge of finding a way out of the Baltics security predicament. It is worth noting that large parts of the policy suggestions of this RAND report now seem to have been incorporated in the United States policy towards the Baltic region. At a meeting of senior EU and American officials in Brussels in November 1996, Washington clearly made the case for early EU-entry of those countries that will not join NATO in the first instance.[33] EU member states and the European Commission have responded negatively to these proposals, making it clear that EU membership is no political consolation prize to be given to disappointed Central European countries.

However, the idea of early Estonian EU membership has also found support in Western Europe. For example, Liberal Party chairman and former Danish Foreign Minister Uffe Elleman-Jensen, argued in December 1996: "It is realistic to get one Baltic country in as part of the EU's expansion if there is enough political will. And Estonia is both the smallest and economically best situated of the three countries."[34] Despite (limited) political support for this option, Estonia's entry into the EU will continue to remain problematic for reasons discussed in the previous section (i.e. unresolved minority and border problems). Moreover, one could question whether the suggestion of taking in Estonia (and *ipso facto* leaving out Lithuania and Latvia), will be enthusiastically received in Riga and Vilnius: would this not evoke the same "Korean syndrome" (i.e. that Moscow might assume that Lithuania and Latvia fall outside NATO's direct "sphere of interest") that the authors guard for were *all three* Baltic states left out? These are questions which are difficult to answer as long as Russia has not come to terms with the sovereignty of the Baltic states and as long as Moscow is principally opposed to NATO enlargement as such.

In line with the RAND report, the United states has also made proposals to establish a so-called "PfP-plus" for non-first wave NATO candidate countries. This would be a sort of "super-partnership" strengthening the practical military cooperation along the current PfP-lines, and is intended to blur the differences between membership and non-membership – with the exception, of course, of the formal Article 5 security guarantees. The decision (at the NATO Foreign Ministers meeting on 10 December 1996), to establish a so-called Atlantic Partnership Council (which will presumably see the light in July 1997), is another effort to assure that non-NATO members will have sufficient opportunities to consolidate and strengthen their political and military ties with the Alliance.

In the meantime, Russia's opposition to these developments remains unchanged. Alexander Lebed, in his short-lived capacity as the Kremlin's security chief, declared in the summer of 1996 that Moscow would not oppose NATO enlargement and that "Russia simply cannot be aggressive any more. We have exhausted our appetite for wars. We do not want to fight any more." Adding that "Russia is not planning to fight anyone. (. . .) So this mighty NATO fist is being developed to do battle with the air."[35] But given the Russian tradition to look at the military capabilities of countries and alliances, rather than to take their stated political objectives at face value, it is most likely that Moscow will continue to object to NATO enlargement, especially if it would reach its state borders. In this context it is especially disconcerting that Moscow now seems to require a Western commitment to exclude the Baltic states from the Alliance as a condition for a Russian "endorsement" of NATO's enlargement towards Poland, Hungary, the Czech Republic and Slovakia (and/or Slovenia).[36]

Former British Foreign Secretary Douglas Hurd suggested in May 1996 to establish what he called a "Baltic security sub-zone". This could imply creating a security alliance (including the Baltic states) in which Sweden and Finland would take the lead (perhaps including other Nordic states such as Denmark and Norway).[37] This proposal is said to have some support in Bonn and Moscow. An informal and unpublished US working paper on Baltic security has also made proposals along these lines (designating Sweden as a "guarantor" of Baltic regional security). During his visit to Washington, Swedish Prime Minister Persson outlined a five-part plan to incorporate the Baltic states in Europe's security structure: (1) more bilateral activities among countries in the Baltic area; (2) enhanced regional cooperation among all Scandinavian and Baltic countries; (3) eventual EU membership for the Baltic states; (4) more programmes for military training and border control under NATO's PfP initiative; and (5) an increased dialogue with Russia.[38] Russia might well see this option as a possible compromise to assure, at a minimum, a sort of non-aligned status for the Baltic states. It is, however, questionable whether this "security sub-zone" will be more than a wider and more ambitious Baltic Council. Although Sweden has championed a new approach to Baltic security, it has also made it clear that its policy of neutrality does not include making military commitments to the Baltics. What is more, the Baltic states themselves know all too well that they need more than their Nordic neighbors to balance a potentially resurgent imperialistic Russia.

Another alternative would be that the Baltic states would be identified by the EU, WEU and NATO as so-called "second wave"- countries, which would imply that after the first round of enlargement a number of Central European countries would be listed as potential new members. Lithuanian Defense Minister Linas Linkevicius argued during the Nordic and Baltic Defense summit of June 1996, that NATO should give the Baltic states the status of "Future Candidates."[39] He later added that "what matters to us is continuity of the [NATO enlargement] process. We need to see clear positions, clear signals and clear and specific political decisions which would signify that this will not be the last train. We want to know that the first railway carriage [to get NATO] will definitely not be the last one."[40] Such a "signal" might be little more than a symbolic gesture, but the granting of the status of "Future Candidate, or even "Future Member", might well be a means for overcoming the Baltic fear of being left on their own in a grey security area.

The OSCE: a quiet moderator

The weaknesses of the OSCE are well-know to all students of international affairs: it is an unwieldy, under-institutionalized and under-funded organization of 55 member states without mechanisms to implement most of its own decisions. At the same time, the accomplishments of the OSCE are generally overlooked, although the OSCE does certainly have a number of successes. Over the past few years, the OSCE has tried to develop new concepts and methods with a view to preventing the outbreak of armed conflicts. It has set up the services of a High Commissioner on National Minorities (HCNM) for the purposes of early detection and defusion of (potential) conflicts involving minorities. The HCNM was established in December 1992 and has already made significant contributions to lessening tensions in some Central European countries and in parts of the former USSR.

In the Baltic region, the main task of the HCNM (former Dutch Minister of Foreign Affairs Max van der Stoel) has been to find an acceptable compromise between Estonia and Russia, and between Latvia and Russia. The High Commissioner has undertaken a number of missions to both Baltic republics, especially dealing with questions relating to the Russian-speaking minority and civil rights legislation (citizenship). The HCNM acts under the aegis of the OSCE Senior Council and during his mission the High Commission makes contact with all interested parties (i.e. Governments, political parties and non-governmental organizations), and draws up a confidential report that makes concrete and practical recommendations to alleviate or solve the problem. The low profile of the High Commissioner should be regarded as a key asset, since in almost all cases the parties involved in the conflict are asked to change their positions and compromise. High publicity and full media coverage, combined with public report by the HCNM, would not be conducive to such a delicate process.

The OSCE has also established a so-called Long Term Mission in Estonia, which started its work on 15 February 1993. The objective of this Mission is to "further promote integration and better understanding between the communities in Estonia." The Terms of Reference contained, among others, the following elements: (1) establish and maintain contacts with competent authorities on both the national and the local level, in particular with those responsible for citizenship, migration, language questions, social services and employment; (2) collect information and serve as a clearing-house for information, technical assistance and advice on matters relating to the status of the communities in Estonia and the rights and duties of their members; and (3) contribute to the efforts of Estonian national and local authorities to re-create a civic society, *inter alia* through the promotion of local mechanisms to facilitate dialogue and understanding. A similar OSCE Mission started its work in Latvia (with slightly more limited Terms of Reference) on 19 November 1993. The size of these missions is very limited (6 members in Estonia, 4 in Latvia), with an equally modest budget. The Missions are usually established for a period of six months with subsequent prolongations.

In taking this intermediary position, the OSCE plays the role of a quite moderator between those Baltic republics with significant Russian minorities and Russia proper. In doing so, the OSCE is going places where neither NATO nor the EU/WEU can (or want to) go. Russia and the Baltic states are all member states of the OSCE and can conduct a dialogue and negotiate on contentious problems on an equal footing. Quite understandably, most Baltic policy makers and analysts remain skeptical about Russia's efforts to strengthen and reform the OSCE. From a Baltic perspective, Russia seems intent on using the OSCE to carve out its own exclusive sphere of interests and making NATO subordinate to a vague and most likely teeth- and powerless pan-European security organization. As one Latvian observer stated recently: "It is clear that Russia is trying to bolster those organizations which are unable to provide sufficient security guarantees for the new European nations and also to influence the one organization which could become a security guarantor for the new countries (NATO) in a way which is favorable to Russia."[41] Although the OSCE obviously has an important role to play in preventive diplomacy and conflict prevention, it lacks the facet which is most attractive for the Baltic states: a clear-cut Western security guarantee.

For the moment, therefore, the role of the OSCE is a modest one. The principal reason for the OSCE's marginal role is that conflict prevention is fine in theory, but notoriously difficult to put in practice. Early identification and analysis of a problem is crucial to the prevention of a conflict, but this does not automatically mean that European and American policy makers will invest the political energy and capital trying to douse the flames. As Jonathan Eyal stated in 1994: "No [Western] politician has won votes by claiming to have prevented a conflict which, by definition, never existed because it was prevented. In electoral terms, convincing politicians to invest in conflict prevention is like asking a teenager to save for a pension."[42] Eyal's remark is to the point: it remains a fact that the "international community" which is at times evoked does not exist; there are only nation states and alliances with their own foreign policy agendas and national interests. For that reason, the Baltic states have been lukewarm toward OSCE-involvement in their countries, despite the fact that the quiet moderation of the OSCE has added in practical terms considerably to their security and stability, and perhaps even more than other European security organizations.

Concluding remarks

During the years to come the role and place of the Baltic states in Europe's security framework will remain unclear. The question of how the Baltic states should be integrated in Europe's security institutions without antagonizing Russia has not yet been answered satisfactorily. For reasons indicated earlier, the RAND option (EU membership of Estonia without WEU and NATO membership) has some serious drawbacks and does not seem to be widely supported by EU member states.

For the moment, the Baltic states are taking full advantage of their geographical position as the relatively well-organized and safe hub for Western investors interested in the huge Russian and former-Soviet market. But at the same time they continue to suffer from what may be called Europe's institutional enlargement "mortgage"-paradox: Most banks are keen to give a mortgage to wealthy clients but are usually less forthcoming to poor clients who need it most. So with the EU/WEU and NATO: those countries whose security is less firmly based and most fragile are most in need to be anchored in Europe's security institutions, but for the same reasons they have less of a chance to join than stable and balanced democracies such as the Czech Republic and Poland. The enlargement policies of the EU/WEU and NATO are certainly prudent and based on a sound, rational strategy: the need to maintain the internal cohesion of Europe's institutions, to guard against any serious dilution of their operational capacities and to make sure that enlargement will not invoke serious rebuttals from powerful neighboring countries which would undermine the development of a cooperative European security system. But at the same time one might question such prudence and call for a bolder, less intrepid, strategy that would use the window of opportunity as long as it is still open.

To a certain extent, the most likely future candidate countries of the EU, WEU and NATO (i.e. the Czech Republic, Hungary and Poland) all find themselves in a similar quandary as the Baltic states. But on top of that, the Baltic states are widely considered as militarily "undefensible": they are small, flat and lack the necessary strategic depth. This should, however, not be considered an insurmountable obstacle. In this context, Latvian Ambassador Valdis Krastins has made a parallel with the allegedly "undefensible" strategic position of Berlin during the Cold War, reminding us that the Soviets backed down after "decisive Allied actions".[43] It has also been argued that the Baltic states only have "CNN defence", that is that they can only resist for as long as possible in the hope that global television will generate sufficient Western public support. In this context Douglas Hurd asked in April 1996: "Is it really credible that the United States, or indeed Britain, would undertake to defend Estonia if this could only be done with nuclear weapons?"[44] No doubt the answer to this question is an unequivocal No. But then again, would Washington (or indeed London or Paris) be prepared to defend Turkey in the very unlikely case that this could only be done with nuclear weapons? One might even question the utility and reliability of the American nuclear umbrella over the NATO area as a whole now that Europe is facing new and more diverse security challenges in which the practical utility of nuclear weapons is very limited indeed.

But raising the issue of the (difficult) defensibility of the Baltic states as an argument for excluding these countries from the first (and/or second) wave of enlargement may well miss the key point, namely that the consolidation of Baltic independence should be one of the central Western political and strategic interests. Former Swedish Prime Minister Carl Bildt has correctly argued that "Russia's policies toward the Baltic countries will be the litmus test of its new direction", and that Russia's conduct towards these states will show the true nature of Russia's commitment to international norms and principles."[45] Bildt has further argued that addressing the security predicament of the Baltic states also poses "a test of the potential of European institutions to identify and solve conflicts before they develop into major problems."[46] It is generally acknowledged that the West has limited influence over Russia's policies towards Central Asia and the Caucasus, but that the ability of Western policy to affect developments in the Baltic region is considerable. It should be made clear that despite Russia's understandable security concerns in the Baltic region, Moscow should realize that what it calls its "near abroad" is also an area of significant strategic interest for the West. By restraining Russia's policy towards the Baltic region, for example by clearly identifying the three Baltic states as "Future Candidates" or "Future Members" of the EU, WEU and NATO (an option discussed above), the West will send a clear signal to Moscow without provoking counterproductive and potentially destabilizing reactions. At the same time it will encourage in Russia the development of a non-imperialistic and non-expansionist national security strategy and self-image, which in itself is a prerequisite for integrating Russia in Europe's evolving security framework.

Notes

1 *FBIS − WEU − 96 − 246*, 19 December 1996.
2 Alois Mock, "Austria's Role in the New Europe", *NATO Review*, Vol. 43, No. 2 (March 1995), p. 17 (emphasis added).
3 See Peter van Ham, "Prospects for Membership of Central European Countries in the European Union", in Finn Laursen and Søren Riishøj (eds.), *The EU and Central Europe: Status and Prospects* (Esbjerg: South Jutland University Press, 1997).
4 See Peter van Ham, "Central Europe and the EU's Intergovernmental Conference: The Dialectics of Enlargement", in *Security Dialogue* (Vol. 28, No. 1, March 1997).
5 *Financial Times*, 17 June 1996.
6 *Estonia, Latvia and Lithuania: EIU Country Report*, The Economist Intelligence Unit, 2nd quarter 1996.
7 See Atis Lejins and Daina Bleiere (eds), *The Baltic States. Search For Security*, (Riga: Latvian Institute of International Affairs, 1996); Atis Lejins and Paulis Apinis (eds), *The Baltic States on Their Way to the European Union*, (Riga: Latvian Institute of International Affairs with the Konrad Adenauer Stiftung, 1995); Peter van Ham (ed), *The Baltic States. Security and Defence After Independence*, (Paris: Chaillot Paper 19, WEU Institute for Security Studies, June 1995); and Erkki Nordberg, *The Baltic Republics. A Strategic Survey*, (Helsinki: Finnish Defence Studies, National Defence College, 1994).
8 See on the relations between Estonia and Russia: Graeme Herd with Ene Rôngelep and Anton Surikov, *Crisis For Estonia? Russia, Estonia and a*

Post-Chechen Cold War, London Defence Studies 29, The Centre for Defence Studies, London, September 1995.

9 *The Baltic Times*, 21–7 March 1996.

10 See for a comprehensive overview on this issue Wendell H. Kadunce, *Baltic-Nordic Relations. Implications for Baltic Security*, Berichte des Bundesinstituts für ostwissenschaftliche und international Studien, (September 1995).

11 In the summer of 1997, Denmark will hand over coordination of Baltbat to the Baltic states themselves. It is the intention to develop Baltbat into an infantry brigade armed with light armament, complemented by anti-tank and anti-aircraft defence weapons

12 *FBIS – WEU – Daily Report*, 4 November 1996.

13 *FBIS – WEU – Daily Report*, 6 December 1996.

14 Colonel Juris Dalbins, "Baltic Cooperation – The Key to Wider Security", in *NATO Review*, January 1996.

15 *Together in Europe. European Union Newsletter for Central Europe*, No. 90 (1 June 1996).

16 *FBIS – SOV – Daily Report*, 26 November 1996.

17 *FBIS – SOV – Daily Report*, 27 August 1996.

18 *FBIS – SOV – Daily Report*, 14 October 1996.

19 *Together in Europe*, No. 86 (1 April 1996).

20 Saulius Girnius, "Relations With Russia Turn Bitter", in *Transition*, Vol. 2, No. 11, 31 May 1996.

21 Anatol Lieven, "Baltic Iceberg Dead Ahead: NATO Beware", in *The World Today*, July 1996.

22 Peter van Ham, *The EC, Eastern Europe and European Unity*, (London: Pinter Publishers, 1993).

23 See for one of the few exceptions: D. Danilov, *Post-Maastricht Western Europe. The Development of Integration in the Security Sector* (in Russian), (Moscow, Institute of Europe, 1994).

24 *Russia and NATO. Theses of the Council on Foreign and Defense Policy*, (1995), point 2.3.6 which refers to the "Enlargement of WEU in the first turn" (i.e. the autonomous enlargement of WEU towards Central Europe).

25 Although there is some support for this idea in the US. See Jonathan Dean, "Losing Russia or Keeping NATO – Must We Choose?", in *Arms Control Today*, (June 1995), p. 7, and "Should NATO Grow? – A Dissent" (An open letter to the editor by R.T. Davies), *The New York Review of Books*, 3 May 1995.

26 *Study on NATO Enlargement*, (Brussels: NATO Office of Information and Press, September 1995); and M. Rühle and N. Williams, "NATO Enlargement an the European Union", in *The World Today*, (May 1995).

27 *WEU Contribution to the European Union Intergovernmental Conference of 1996*, adopted at the WEU Council of Ministers in Madrid, on 14 November 1995.

28 *The IGC and the Security and Defence Dimension – Towards an Enhanced EU Role in Crisis Management*, joint Finnish-Swedish memorandum (25 April 1996).

29 *The Baltic Times*, 28 March – 3 April 1996.

30 *The Baltic Times*, 20 – 26 June 1996.

31 *Financial Times*, 3 May 1996.
32 Ronald D. Asmus and Robert C. Nurick, "NATO Enlargement and the Baltic States", in *Survival*, Vol. 38, No. 2 (Summer 1996).
33 *The Guardian*, 25 November 1996.
34 *FBIS – WEU – Daily Report*, 22 December 1996.
35 *International Herald Tribune*, 19 June 1996, and *Financial Times*, 25 July 1996.
36 Zbigniew Brzezinski, "Russia: Terms for Accommodation With an Expanded NATO", *International Herald Tribune*, 22 August 1996; and Jim Hoagland, "Expand the European Union Instead of NATO", *International Herald Tribune*, 5 August 1996.
37 *Financial Times*, 3 May 1996.
38 *International Herald Tribune*, 10–11 August 1996, and *FBIS – WEU – Daily Report*, 7 August 1996.
39 *The Baltic Times*, 6–12 June 1996.
40 *FBIS – SOV – Daily Report*, 25 September 1996.
41 Aivars Stranga, "Russia and the Security of the Baltic States: 1991–1996", in Lejins and Bleiere (eds), *The Baltic States*, p. 174.
42 Jonathan Eyal, "No One Cares Until It's War", in *The Independent*, 10 March 1994.
43 *International Herald Tribune*, 6 December 1996.
44 Quoted in *The Economist*, 4 May 1996. In July 1996, Vladimir Lukin, chairman of the Russian Duma's foreign affairs committee stated before a Baltic audience: "But you realize that no European country will enter a war against Russia for the Baltics. This is why you should not be invited to NATO." See *The Baltic Times*, 4–10 July 1996.
45 Carl Bildt, "The Baltic Litmus Test", in *Foreign Affairs*, (Vol. 73, No. 5, September/October 1994), p. 72.
46 Carl Bildt, "Watch Russia's Baltic 'Near Abroad'", in *International Herald Tribune*, 27 July 1993.

Chapter 3

The Baltic States in Post-Cold War U.S. Strategy[1]

Stuart J. Kaufman

According to Clinton Administration rhetoric, the U.S. national security strategy in Europe is a liberal one. Aimed at building a prosperous, cooperative peace throughout the continent, the strategy focuses on promoting democracy on the eastern half of the continent, and on integrating all of Europe into West European and Atlantic economic, political and security institutions. American policy toward the Baltic states is part of this same strategy, emphasizing cooperation, reassurance and engagement. Applied in an atmosphere of broad and growing acceptance of liberal norms in Europe, and in the absence of any significant threat of overt military aggression, such a policy of liberal institution-building ought to be a promising one. The continuing drive to expand NATO, however, contradicts the rest of the policy, and in combination with increasingly assertive Russian nationalism, it threatens to re-divide Europe rather than uniting it.

In fact, in the Baltic region, the policies of all the main players – the U.S., Russia, and the Baltic countries themselves – are based more on the Realist logic of geopolitical competition than on the liberal logic of cooperative institution-building. Those policies, especially including the drive to expand NATO eastward, are as a result increasingly working to reawaken the security dilemma in the eastern part of Europe. The U.S., by proclaiming that NATO expansion – that is, the expansion of its own sphere of influence – is necessary to stabilize and reassure the East-Central Europeans, implies that the Baltic states, too, could best be stabilized and reassured by NATO membership.

[1] The author would like to thank the participants in the conference, "The Baltic States in Global Politics," for ideas and insights which have greatly contributed to improving this essay. The contributions of Drs. Gunnar Arteus, Birthe Hansen, Bertel Heurlin, Olav Knudsen, and Alexander Pikayev are particularly acknowledged.

The Balts, inclined to fear Russian imperial tendencies anyway, build on this rhetoric and proclaim that their security can *only* be assured by NATO membership, exacerbating the security fears of their citizens as long as they are excluded. The Russians, in an increasingly assertive nationalist mood anyway, correctly interpret any NATO expansion as the expansion of an opposing sphere of influence, despite Western claims that it is not. For both sets of reasons – its own revanchist mood and its concern about expanding Western influence – Russia feels increasingly insecure, and therefore increasingly inclined to try to re-establish its own influence by whatever heavy-handed methods may be required. In short, the cost of NATO expansion in East-Central Europe is to exacerbate insecurity in the states north and east of the Nieman.

In this chapter I explore the implications of this dilemma. I begin with a discussion of my theoretical point of departure, which depends on taking into account both Realist and neoliberal instutionalist arguments about the nature of international politics. Building on this discussion, I proceed with an analysis of American security policy toward Europe in general and the Baltic states in particular, showing how American policy is a contradictory mix of both Realist and neoliberal initiatives. I then consider the effects of the security policies of the Baltic states themselves, which tend in many ways to exacerbate the contradictory nature of U.S. and NATO policy. Finally, I turn to the implications of these policies for Russian security, and the effects of Russian policy on Baltic security. In the conclusion, I argue that the security dilemma which emerges for both Russia and the Baltic states may not be resolvable in the context of current NATO policies. The best chance is to try to construct a cooperative security regime in the Baltic or Nordic region which would alleviate security concerns on all sides, but the push to expand NATO may make such a regime unworkable.

Theoretical grounding

The main point of departure in this chapter is the idea summed up in the title of an article by Alexander Wendt: "Anarchy is what states make of it" (Wendt 1992). My assumption is that even though the international system is largely (though not entirely) anarchic, that anarchy does not necessarily require that states engage in a continuous struggle for power and survival. If a number of leading states do embark on such a competition, the others are forced to do so in self-defense. However, if the leading powers in the system consider such power struggles illegitimate or inappropriate, they can construct a system which punishes such behavior, creating strong incentives for states to keep their competition moderate and non-violent. In short, contrary to the neorealist argument offered by Waltz (1979) and his followers, anarchy does not *require* that states engage in geopolitical competition; it merely permits them to do so. If they choose to do so, it is because of reasons internal to the states, reasons of the sort suggested by classical Realists such as Morgenthau (1967). Buzan, Jones and Little (1993) show, in contrast, that some historical international systems have been characterized by norms of cooperation or limited competition – in short, by the sort of behavior hypothesized in neoliberal institutionalist theory (Keohane and Nye 1977), and by earlier "idealists" – rather than by the behavior hypothesized by Realists or neorealists.

My theoretical assumption, in short, is that if leading states choose to act the way Realists expect them to act, then the system will be one well-described by Realist theory; but if they act according to norms which, for example, consider major war to be essentially obsolete (Mueller 1989), they can make it so. These norms act both by moderating individual states' policies, and by underpinning the international regimes or international "society" (see, e.g., Bull 1977), which, structured by international institutions, help maintain an essentially peaceful system. The security dilemma, in this peaceful system, is not abolished; it is avoided – that is, states avoid posing threats to each other for normative reasons, so each feels unthreatened by the actions of the others. Such a system can only exist, however, if peaceful norms are widespread enough that serious challenges to the system are extremely rare. If a number of states engage in geopolitical competition which creates the threat of violent conflict, security dilemmas inevitably re-emerge and the system comes to be characterized by Realist logic. The peaceful system lasts, in short, only as long as the consensus among major states which makes it possible.

American strategy for Europe and the Baltic Region

According to the Clinton Administration's basic strategy document, entitled *A National Security Strategy of Engagement and Enlargement*, U.S. strategy both worldwide and in Europe is based on three fundamental components: marrying a strong defense capability to the promotion of cooperative security measures; working to open foreign markets to spur global economic growth; and promoting democracy worldwide (White House 1995, 2–3). All three elements are linked. Based on the assumption that democracies do not fight with one another, the American strategy is to promote democratization. For the same reason, it also aims to help stabilize existing democracies, especially the newer ones, by removing economic and security threats which might undermine fragile democratic institutions, and by promoting open economies and cooperative security arrangements which reinforce democratic governance. At this most general level, the apparent idealism of U.S. policy is genuine, and indeed is typical of American foreign policy thinking. The U.S. genuinely aims to create a peaceful international system stabilized by liberal (peaceful and capitalist) norms and by international institutions.

Regarding Europe, the security aspects of American policy – both the "engagement" and the "enlargement" dimensions – have been focused through NATO and its "Partnership for Peace" (PfP) program. According to the Defense Department, PfP "is already extending a zone of stability eastward across Europe and Central Asia by promoting military cooperation among . . . countries in the region". The centerpiece of the program is a series of joint exercises which, according to the Secretary of Defense, "have had a remarkable effect on European security by building confidence, promoting transparency, and reducing tensions" even between long-time rivals, as the 1996 Romanian-Hungarian *rapprochement* illustrates. Additionally, in the Secretary's view, "many Partner nations have accelerated" political and economic reforms because they are "a prerequisite to participation in PfP or membership in NATO" (Perry 1996, xii-xiii). The same mechanism is also being used to manage U.S.-Russian security cooperation: the Pentagon says that it aims "to encourage Russia to play a constructive role in the new European security architecture through the development of NATO-Russia relations and through Russia's active participation in PfP" (Perry 1996, 3).

A State Department policy statement (1996) shows how the U.S. has tried to apply these principles to its policy in the Baltic region. Principal U.S. policy goals have been "the orderly withdrawal of Russian troops from the region, Baltic integration into Western political, economic and security structures, and the strengthening of bilateral ties," all based on the assumption that "stable, democratic, prosperous and secure Baltic nations are key to regional peace". The Administration points to a range of specific programs aimed at promoting these goals. In the economic field, the U.S. has reached a series of agreements with the Baltic states on trade and investment, and it has encouraged creation of a "Baltic-American Enterprise Fund" which helps promote U.S.-Baltic trade links. In the area of political integration, the U.S. has supported Baltic membership in the Council of Europe, the European Union, and other institutions. And in the security area, the document points to a number of measures including financial assistance for housing Russian officers withdrawn from the region, direct provision of military supplies, joint peace-keeping exercises and security consultative arrangements under PfP, Baltic participation in the NATO-led Bosnian Implementation Force, and a Regional Airspace Initiative.

In the fall of 1996, administration officials presented to the Baltic governments a "Baltic Action Plan" to promote security in the region. The plan reportedly included three elements: U.S. aid in helping the Baltic states meet NATO membership requirements; an emphasis on the importance of good relations between the Baltic states and Russia; and bilateral charters on economic, political and security cooperation (*Estonian Review*, 9 – 15 September 1996). These initiatives also fit with the general "strategy of engagement and enlargement": its elements were aimed at promoting the engagement of the Baltic states both with NATO and with Russia, at the same time promoting at least notionally the enlargement of NATO institutions to improve security in the region.

Together, this array of liberal institutionalist initiatives is supposed to address all of the kinds of security threats – "hard" external threats as well "soft" and internal security threats – which might face the Baltic states (see Heurlin 1996, 75–80). Regarding internal threats, cooperation with PfP is meant to mitigate any possible threat of *coups d'etat* by improving civil-military relations and officer training, while membership in the Council of Europe should mitigate any threat of domestic unrest by promoting human rights and the improvement of democratic institutions. Regarding external threats – meaning primarily the possibility of renewed Russian expansionism – the idea is to enmesh Russia in a set of institutions which will ensure that Russian interests are best secured by cooperative engagement with the West rather than by neo-imperialist expansion. The second element of the "Baltic Action Plan" has the related goal of pushing Russia and the Baltic states to settle outstanding issues by negotiation rather than allowing them to escalate into serious security disputes.

The biggest flaw in this policy is its inclusion of plans for the eastward expansion of NATO, which is likely to promote more geopolitical competition than liberal integration. The Clinton Administration claims that NATO expansion is simply another case of liberal institution-building: "NATO expansion will not be aimed at replacing one division of Europe with a new one, but to enhance the security of all European states, members and non-members alike" (White House 1995, p. 27). By all appearances, the administration and its apologists actually believe this claim: as President Clinton put it, "I came to office convinced that NATO can do for Europe's East what it did for Europe's West: prevent a return to local rivalries, strengthen democracy against future threats, and create the conditions for prosperity to flourish" (Clinton 1996). On the basis of such logic, the Clinton Administration is moving toward expanding NATO membership to a group of East-Central European countries – primarily Poland, the Czech Republic, and Hungary – by 1999.

The real logic of this policy, however, is not liberal but geopolitical or Realist. The U.S. claims that NATO expansion is desirable because new members will be protected from "instability" – that is, that inclusion in the NATO sphere will help stabilize fragile democratic governments, secure new members against any external military threat, and ensure NATO management of any intramural squabbles they have among themselves. There is some truth to this claim: association with NATO probably does provide some increment of "soft" security for candidate members, and the very prospect of membership has motivated states such as Romania and Hungary to compose their differences (Bailes 1997). But overall, this argument is more smokescreen than honest explanation: there is little evidence that NATO membership stabilizes democratic governments or prevents conflicts among members – witness Greece and Turkey on both counts – and the candidates for immediate membership face no current external security threats (see Brown 1995).

The real reason the states of East-Central Europe (and the Baltic region) want NATO membership is that they fear future threats from Russia, so they want "hard" security guarantees to deter any such future Russian attack. In short, they wish to be included in an American sphere of influence so they can avoid inclusion in a Russian one. While the U.S. insists that NATO expansion is not creating a new "division of Europe," it is doing precisely that, underlining the difference between NATO members and non-members by adding some countries but not others. Such a new division is impermissible if the liberal vision of European security is to prevail: what is needed, in such a case, is to create a pan-European collective *security* system including Russia. This can be done either by transforming NATO into such an institution, or more conservatively by building collective security around another institution (such as OSCE), and allowing NATO – a collective *defense* arrangement – slowly to wither away if the larger institution is effective.

The current NATO tack – expansion of NATO as a military bloc which will continue to exclude Russia – undermines the liberal vision. As long as NATO maintains its character as a military bloc, no special NATO-Russia relationship can change the fact that modest NATO expansion re-divides Europe and constitutes a potential security threat to Russia. From the Russian point of view, NATO expansion to Poland means arrangements for the forward basing of NATO military power, most ominously air power, nearly a thousand kilometers closer to Moscow. Given Russia's disintegrating air defense system, Russia is increasingly unable either to defend itself against potential attack by such forward-based aircraft or to respond in kind; it would therefore face the alternatives of nuclear retaliation or no response at all. This is precisely the sort of "humiliation or holocaust" scenario which motivated the American side in the arms race of the early 1980s. Regardless of the political unlikelihood of any such attack, NATO's character as a military bloc forces Russian security policy makers to take into account the military possibility, and find some military answer to it. Thus NATO eastward expansion creates a security dilemma for Russia – and for NATO itself once Russia has responded – thereby undermining the sort of cooperative security system NATO countries claim to want to build.

Furthermore, while President Clinton asserts that "a gray zone of insecurity must not re-emerge in Europe," his policy of stepwise expansion ensures the emergence of just such a zone, including most significantly the Baltic states and Ukraine. The threat to Russian interests posed by an expanding NATO inevitably increases Russian temptations to respond by establishing a sphere of influence in those states – especially the CIS countries and the Baltic states – which are excluded from the NATO zone.

Faced with this obvious cost to Baltic security, the U.S. Administration has been forced to perform a complicated dance regarding the question of Baltic inclusion in NATO. On one side, since it has been treating NATO as simply another international institution with a particular set of objective membership criteria, the Administration has been forced into the stance that the Baltic states are "fully eligible" for

NATO membership in the future, once they have met the criteria (*OMRI Daily Report*, 10 October 1996). On the other hand, recognizing that NATO is not simply another institution, but a solemn commitment to mutual defense, the Administration has refused to specify the membership criteria, arguing one day that the barrier to Baltic state membership was their military weakness, and literally the next day that the problem was outstanding disputes with Russia (*Monitor*, 26 September 1996 and 27 September 1996). The point, of course, is to avoid being trapped once the Baltic states can say, "We have met the requirements. Now let us in".

The Administration has a number of other reasons for its tap dance as well. The first is domestic political pressure. NATO expansion has emerged as the trendy position *du jour* for those American politicians who wish to appear "tough on defense"; thus the U.S. House of Representatives voted in July 1996 to call for NATO membership for Poland, the Czech Republic, and Hungary, authorizing $60 million in aid to help those countries prepare for membership (*OMRI Daily Report*, 24 July 1996). Opposition Presidential candidate Robert Dole, traditionally responsive to domestic pressure groups in U.S. foreign policy, went even further, calling for inclusion of the Baltic states in a second round of NATO expansion (*Monitor*, 26 June 1996). On this issue, however, even U.S. hawks disagree: the Heritage Foundation, a usually hard-line think-tank, contends that "The U.S. does not have the capability or will to offer iron-clad security guarantees" to the Baltic states (Holmes and Moore 1996, p. 25).

In this context, the Administration was able to implement its preferred election strategy of "triangulation," distancing itself from the extremes of both parties and occupying what appears to be the political center. Thus President Clinton called for some expansion of NATO, insulating himself from further Congressional pressure, and his mentioning of a specific target date created the appearance of "leadership" on the issue. At the same time, he distanced himself from the "extremists" – conveniently putting opponent Dole in the "extremist" category – by refusing to make any promises to the Baltic states, secure in his assurance that even many conservatives were on his side. Even better, the policy buffered Clinton from criticism from the pro-Baltic lobby by insisting that the Baltic states were eligible for consideration for NATO membership in the future.

Yet another reason for the Administration's vagueness on the Baltic issue is its desire to extract some positive benefit from the security "gray zone" it is reluctantly creating. Thus while refusing to make any firm security guarantee to the Baltic states, the Administration does label the security of the Baltic states to be "of direct and material interest to the United States". The promotion of security cooperation through PfP is aimed at the same goal: the creation of some weak "general deterrence" of any Russian attack by refusing to promise *not* to intervene in case of conflict. This is in part the result of lessons from two of the United States's most costly foreign policy failures: the oubreak of the conflicts in Korea and the Persian Gulf. In both cases, U.S. officials had given an apparently clear signal that the U.S. would not get involved in case of conflict – in Secretary of State Dean Acheson's 1950 speech excluding Korea from the American security zone, and in Ambassador April Glaspie's 1990 statement that the U.S. had "no opinion on inter-Arab disputes". Such statements may in both cases have been seen by the aggressors as a "green light" to attack, and they also opened both Administrations to a great deal of domestic criticism.

The policy ambiguity also reflects a genuine uncertainty within the U.S. As with South Korea in 1950 and Kuwait in 1990, the U.S. government considers it extremely unlikely that the U.S. would make a firm commitment to the armed defense of the Baltic states. Indeed, the U.S. has no intrinsic security interests at stake there at all. Nevertheless, such a commitment is not impossible. The proper combination of Russian aggressive behavior and Russian military weakness could well provoke American military intervention. Successful Russian conquest or subversion of the Baltic states would probably provoke a vigorous U.S. response, but one short of the use of armed force. A botched Russian attempt at such invasion or subversion, however, could well provoke American military intervention, depending on circumstances. The current isolationist mood in the United States would militate against such intervention – Trent Lott, the new Senate Majority Leader, is for example openly indifferent to foreign policy (Friedman 1996) – but Russian military aggression is just the sort of event which could spark a resurgence of American foreign involvement. Since the U.S. does not know its own mind on the matter, ambiguity is the best course – though not, as will be discussed below, a costless one.

Barring that sort of Russian blunder, however, future Baltic inclusion in NATO is unlikely, for several reasons (Asmus and Nurick 1996). One is the broader regional impact. The Baltic states would be very difficult to defend, so bases in Sweden might become indispensable to provide the strategic depth necessary to mount such a defense, especially to aid in controlling the Baltic Sea. But Sweden would probably be reluctant to join NATO for historical reasons, and would particularly resist joining without including Finland as well. Including all five Baltic countries, however, would multiply the effects of the expansion enormously: NATO would now have some 2000 km of border with Russia – extremely difficult for NATO defend, and extraordinarily provocative to Russia if it were adequately defended.

A second reason is cost, and the related issue of public willingness to pay. While NATO expansion to East-Central Europe alone might cost a mere $3 – 4 billion per year for 10 – 15 years, spread across all NATO members (Asmus et al. 1996, p. 7), inclusion of three or five Baltic countries would cost much more. East-Central Europe, lacking a long border with Russia, needs no forward deployment of NATO military forces; NATO can therefore rely on preparing for forward deployment in case of need. Estonia, Latvia, and Finland, in constrast, border Russia, so some NATO military deployment on their territories would be essential to block any potential *coup de main*. Thus the financial cost would be substantially greater: NATO would need to maintain more troops; to pay for more forward deployments; and to mount more infrastructure projects and military assistance programs. Additionally, the political effect of placing troops virtually on the border with Russia (meaning anywhere in Latvia or Estonia) would be seen by dovish portions of the public as potentially provocative – especially once Russia made clear how provocative it considered such deployments. The provocation would result in a revival of the Cold War, though at a lower level of threat given Russia's increased weakness relative to the West. It is unclear how much support Western publics would provide to such a policy.

Indeed, the fiscal consequences alone might provoke substantial public opposition. Even in the case of NATO expansion only to East-Central Europe, $3–4 billion in additional expenditures might be hard to find. As increasing social welfare costs threaten Western budgets with growing imbalances, pressure on military budgets is likely to grow, making even maintenance of current, post-Cold War spending levels problematic. In addition, at least in the United States, a deficit of planned defense investment will become severe early in the next century. For example, the average age of U.S. Air Force tactical aircraft will increase by ten years in the decade after 1995, because the U.S. plans virtually no new procurements. In other words, the U.S. today is maintaining high levels of current readiness and capability at the cost of cannibalizing allocations for procurement of new weapons.

Thus the maintenance even of current U.S. force levels will require substantial increases in military procurement costs in the next century as aging weapons systems come to need replacement (Perry 1996, pp. 179–183). It is hard to imagine, in such a fiscal context, a great deal of support for provision of additional security guarantees to strategically marginal and risky areas such as the Baltic states.

Security issues and policies in the Baltic States

One yardstick against which to measure these U.S. policies is the specific array of potential security threats facing the Baltic states. As Barry Buzan (1991) points out, the meaning of "security" goes beyond the issues of protection from external military threat with which Western, and especially U.S., military planners mainly concern themselves. Other security issues, some of which fall under the rubric of "soft" security, include the security of the nation against assimilation or annihilation; the security of the state against *coup d'etat*; and the security of the country's territorial integrity against insurgency by regionally-based minorities. All of these potential problems haunt the Baltic states, especially Estonia and Latvia, and they enormously complicate the problem of promoting security in the Baltic region.

The problem begins with the very existence of the Estonian and Latvian nations. The impulse of the Estonian and Latvian independence movements of the 1980s came largely from a fear that without independence, Russian immigration might eventually lead to the assimilation of all remaining Estonians and Latvians, and the extinction of both nations. When independence was definitively achieved in 1991, it provided not the solution to this problem – most Estonians still perceived a threat of national extinction in 1993 (Kirch and Kirch 1995, p. 51) – but the tools with which the problem could be solved. The policy hit upon in Tallinn and Riga was the political subordination of ethnic Russians as a group, and making full citizenship contingent upon Russian assimilation into the Estonian or Latvian language and (therefore) culture.

This policy, which was aimed at preventing Estonian or Latvian assimilation, helped to create the possibility of other forms of domestic political threat. In Estonia, where much of the Russian population is concentrated in the northeastern corner of the country, there is always the potential for ethnically-based separatism if the Russian population should become sufficiently restive: the first step, a referendum on autonomy in the Russian-inhabited town of Narva, was actually held in July 1993, though further actions were not taken. In Latvia, where the capital city of Riga is largely ethnically Russian, and the Latvians constitute only a bare majority of the country's population, the possibility of a Russian insurgency aimed at gaining political power for that mostly-disfranchised group has to be taken into account. Up to the present, the economic benefits of residence in these countries have led ethnic Russians to accept their lesser political status (Kionka and Vetik 1996). But such acquiescence could change, and the precedents of Moldova, Georgia and Azerbaijan show that Russia is capable of supporting any separatist or insurrectionist impulses which might emerge.

Considered in this context, Latvia and Estonia want NATO membership partly because they want assurance against interference from Moscow with their discrimination against their ethnic Russians. For a long time, politicians in Russia discredited their own protests on this issue by inflating their charges into inaccurate accusations of abuses of "human rights". But this was largely a matter of semantics: what ethnic Russians are deprived of is *civil* rights, and Russian spokesmen are now learning to make this distinction. The shift is significant because it narrows the dispute somewhat: all agree that many ethnic Russians in the Baltic states are denied citizenship in those states, the right to vote in national elections, the unconditional right of residence in their current homes, and so on. Partly because civil rights are at the core of the U.S. civic religion, the United States is reluctant to take on the burden of this dispute – one reason for the reference to "disputes with Russia" as an obstacle to NATO membership for the Balts, and for promotion of "good relations with Russia" as a key element of the "Baltic Action Plan".

The Baltic states do, of course, face security threats for more reasons than their policies toward their Russian minorities. Russia has shown an inclination toward heavy-handed pressure tactics on other issues as well. There is, first, the question of the 1920 treaties between Russia and its Baltic neighbors. Russia's current borders include some land which was recognized in 1920 as parts of Latvia and Estonia, so the Russian government affects a belief that Baltic insistence on recognition of those treaties implies a territorial claim on Russia. The claim is false, since both Latvia and Estonia have made clear a willingness to trade acceptance of the current borders for recognition that the treaties are otherwise valid. The issue is of more than historical interest, because Russian refusal to accept the treaties is based on an insistence that the 1940 Soviet annexations were legal – a position suggesting Russia wishes to maintain the option of using the tactics of 1940 again, implying a threat to the independence of Estonia and Latvia.

Another issue concerns Russian interest in transit rights for purposes including access to ice-free Baltic ports and overland access to the Kaliningrad enclave. The issue of port access may be meant largely as a demand for economic concessions, since the Baltic states are open to trade arrangements with economic benefit to themselves. Alternatively, the problem may be the psychological one of "projection": when the Russians control other countries' export routes – such as Azerbaijan's – they use the resulting leverage to subvert those countries' independence and economic prospects; they obviously wish to foreclose any such leverage being used against themselves. In practice, both motivations probably apply, as Russia attempts to turn a defensive disadvantage into an offensive advantage. Similarly, Russian demands for access to Kaliningrad across Lithuanian territory imply Lithuania's acquiescence in at least an intermittent presence of Russian troops on its territory, a presence Lithuania has historical precedent for fearing. In short, the Baltic states face the problem of fending off incessant Russian political-economic pressure aimed at garnering both economic and geopolitical benefits for Moscow.

The Balts clearly do not do themselves any favors, however, by their inflexible insistence that full NATO membership is the only acceptable means of ensuring their security. The Baltic governments' unanimous denunciation of the "Baltic Action Plan" as a substitute for inclusion in NATO embarrassed a Clinton Administration which will remain their interlocutor in Washington for the next four years. In particular, Estonian President Lennart Meri's intemperate accusation that differentiating between East-Central Europe and the Baltic states was tantamount to a new form of "appeasement" (quoted in Asmus and Nurick 1996, n. 3) can only have harmed his country's case.

Indeed, the Baltic governments' frequent insistence on principle in their policies – on denying citizenship to most ethnic Russians, on recognition of the 1920 treaties, on "equal treatment" as members of "the West" – too often shades into self-righteousness, especially when they deny that principles might be applied to criticize their own behavior as well. Thus they have too often taken the position that because they were not guilty of violations of ethnic Russians' human rights, there was therefore no problem regarding the Russian population at all. Similarly, the Latvian parliament's August 1996 resolution mourning the 1940 loss of territory to Russia constituted precisely the sort of unrealistic territorial claim which can only complicate Baltic-Russian relations (*OMRI Daily Report*, 26 August 1996).

In sum, one of the key difficulties facing U.S. security policy toward the Baltic states is the fact that both Russia and the Balts have legitimate grievances against the other side, so promoting security is not simply a case of defending one side against the unreasonable demands of the other. Rather, both sides have reasonable demands which they take to unreasonable lengths. Promoting dialogue is in principle the best way of handling such disputes, but the approach carries no guarantee of success.

Russian insecurities and Baltic security

A final complication in designing a policy to improve security in the Baltic region is, as has been mentioned above, the problem of ensuring the security of Russia as well as of its neighbors. The possibility of a security dilemma – a situation where one country's improved security comes at the expense of its neighbor's security – is most alive in the possibility of a northward expansion of NATO. No Russian government, however pro-Western in orientation, could fail to be provoked at an expansion of NATO to include the Baltic states – or, even worse, the Baltic states and Finland. Such a shift would constitute the worst geopolitical fears of Russian military planners, as the approaches to Russia's second city would be vulnerable to potential attack on two fronts, from Estonia and from Finland. Thus the Baltic leaders' concept of their own security requirements – full NATO membership or nothing – ensures that either the Baltic states or Russia must remain insecure.

The Russian view that Baltic inclusion in NATO would threaten its security has been repeatedly expressed and codified in Russian policy documents. The 1993 "Basic Provisions of the Russian Federation's Military Doctrine" labelled any "introduction of foreign troops to the territory of states contiguous to the Russian Federation" as "an immediate military threat to the Russian Federation" (*Rossiiskie vesti*, 18 November 1993). By one account the 1995 Russian military doctrine goes even further, stating that if NATO were to expand to include the Baltic states, "then Russian Federation armed forces will immediately be sent into Estonia, Latvia and Lithuania. Any attempt by NATO to prevent this action would be regarded by Russia as the prelude to a worldwide nuclear catastrophe" (*Komsomolskaia pravda*, 29 September 1995). While this statement probably contains a degree of exaggeration for the purposes of deterrence, it provides a useful hint that Baltic inclusion in NATO might spark an irrational Russian reaction. A Yeltsin letter to President Clinton labelling Baltic admission to NATO as an "absolutely unacceptable" move which "would directly challenge Russia's national security interests and undermine European stability and security" (*Monitor*, 3 July 1996) provides a more measured assessment of Russia's views.

Russian policy regarding the expansion of NATO to East-Central Europe, while also a bit variable, has similarly had a consistent theme. The center of the Russian argument is the point that since there is no conceiveable external threat to the Poles, Czechs and Hungarians – Russian military power is too far away – there is no real need for NATO expansion. The general effect of NATO protests about its goals of liberal institution-building is merely to feed Russian cynicism that all such protests merely mask NATO pursuit of geopolitical gains, since in this case such protests *do* work to mask NATO pursuit of geopolitical gains. The Russians are also quite clear that the core of the matter concerns any preparations to implement Article 5 of the treaty: as Foreign Minister Yevgeny Primakov put it, "If new NATO members get fully integrated into the military systems of the Alliance – control, communications, reconnaissance, logistical support, etc. – then to deploy NATO troops on the territories of those countries may be a matter of several hours. Such a contingency . . . would become an uncertainty factor for us" (*Monitor*, 26 July 1996).

Like the Balts, however, the Russians have ensured through their policies that the security dilemma will be more severe than it might be. Constant Russian harping on nonexistent "human rights" abuses, mentioned above, merely fed the fears of the Baltic governments that nothing they did would be considered enough by Russia: they *did* ensure Russians' human rights (if not, again, their civil rights), and they were given no credit for that degree of flexibility. Similarly, Estonia's concession that acceptance of the 1920 treaties need not entail acceptance of the 1920 borders did not evoke similar concessions on the Russian side. If Russia wanted the "territorial claims" question resolved, it could be resolved to Russia's satisfaction. Russia has, instead, refused to take "yes" for an answer in order to maintain a rhetorical club to use against its Baltic neighbors.

Similarly, with regard to NATO expansion to East-Central Europe, Russia has threatened not merely to review the Conventional Forces in Europe treaty, a treaty which is at least logically connected, but also to create a CIS defense community – implicitly, coercively if necessary – and to abrogate nuclear arms control treaties as well. Russia's demand for acquiescing in NATO expansion is the conversion of the alliance essentially into a collective security rather than a collective defense arrangement – one not unlike OSCE, and one in which Russia would have a strong voice and presumably a veto. Russia, in short, demands the impossible and threatens the unreasonable if its demand is not met.

More generally, Russian politicians have in their foreign policy rhetoric increasingly fed a mood of assertive nationalism in Russia which can only be a barrier to improving security relations in Europe. The 1995 military doctrine's threat of nuclear war in case of NATO expansion to the Baltic states was one contribution to this climate by military leaders; the intelligence service has added charges of Western conspiracies aimed at undermining the Russian economy. Other Russian politicians add to the mix territorial claims against Russia's neighbors (with Sevastapol the most popular recent target), charges that any Russian concession is tantamount to "humiliation" or being "spat upon" by the West (a specialty of Alexander Lebed), and so on. The use of military force (directly or by proxy) in Moldova, Georgia, Azerbaijan and Tajikistan, not to mention Chechnya, has been the tangible expression of this aggressive rhetoric, carried out even though polls show little popular support for such measures. The overall effect of this aggressive rhetoric is to create internal pressure on the Russian government to expand Russia's geopolitical influence even in the face of NATO restraint, and to respond vigorously to any suggestion of expansion of NATO's sphere.

Prospects for a cooperative Baltic security regime

In principle, the Baltic region is a suitable location for attempting to create a cooperative security regime. A regime is most commonly defined as commonly accepted "principles, norms, rules and decision-making procedures" (Krasner 1982). A Baltic cooperative security regime would be based on the norms of cooperative security rather than unilateral military efforts to achieve security; principles of neutralization backed by appropriate security guarantees; and rules and procedures embodied in some kind of regional security institution. Indeed, it is American policy, as formulated in the Baltic Action Plan, to promote such institution-building in the region.

Additionally, the Nordic countries, with their longtime commitment to cooperative approaches to security, would be likely to be strong supporters of such a regime. Further, any such arrangement would, by definition, exclude any northward expansion of NATO, and it would therefore be of substantial benefit to Russia. Military arrangements need not deviate substantially from original CFE norms, as long as they banned Russia from massing the force necessary for a *coup de main* against the Baltic states (the recent adjustment in Russia's favor was a step backward in this regard).

The difficulty is that, as of this writing, all of the key actors in the Baltic security puzzle – NATO, Russia, and the Baltic states themselves – are committed to policies incompatible with the establishment of a cooperative security regime in the region. NATO is committed to expansion to East-Central Europe, a policy which undermines Russian faith in the very idea of cooperative security arrangements based on liberal institution-building. Russia, for its part, is committed to a confrontational foreign policy aimed at coercing and controlling its neighbors, trying to use levers such as Baltic treatment of Russian minorities to control Baltic states' policies on a range of issues. And the Balts are inflexible in their demands for early and full admission to NATO, insisting on guarantees current NATO members are not prepared to grant.

What is worse, the current NATO policy of leaving the door open to northward expansion undermines any incentive on the part either of the Baltic states or of Russia to compose their differences. For Russia, a conciliatory policy toward the Baltic states would be its own punishment, as settlement of outstanding disputes with those states would, according to recent U.S. rhetoric, help pave the way for their inclusion in NATO. Thus for Russia, intransigence on all outstanding matters is the course more likely to deter NATO expansion to the region. The Balts, meanwhile, have an incentive to work toward meeting other NATO membership requirements – increasing their defense budgets and so on – while blaming Russian intransigence for the continuing deadlock in their relations with their eastern neighbor, thereby supporting their claim that NATO membership is necessary for their security.

If a cooperative security arrangement in the region is to be possible, it can only occur if NATO policy is aimed at pushing both Russians and Balts to go along. The offer to Russia must be that creation of a cooperative security regime will foreclose northward NATO expansion, while a coercive Russian policy in the region might promote it.

The incentive to the Balts must be that any security guarantee at all – with "soft" guarantees most likely – is dependent on their adopting an accomodating stance toward Russia, their Russian minorities, and the prospect of their security being guaranteed by something less than full NATO membership. There is little reason to believe any of the parties are currently disposed to alter their policy in this direction. The prognosis is therefore that the *status quo* is likely to continue: the Baltic states will continue to pursue a full NATO membership which will continue to elude them, and they will continue to be bullied by Russia.

In this context, the most important factor for Baltic security will be relations between Estonia and Latvia and their Russian minorities. Russia is too deeply enmeshed in the world economy for a shift from political pressure to overt military attack to be a rational policy. For this reason, Moscow's attempts to control its other neighbors (especially in the Transcaucasus) have uniformly relied on local proxies. Therefore, as long as the Baltic Russians are content enough to resist blandishments to become Moscow's proxies, the independence of the Baltic countries is fairly safe.

References

Asmus, Ronald D., Richard L. Kugler and F. Stephen Larrabee. 1996. "What Will NATO Enlargement Cost?". *Survival*, Vol. 38, No. 3 (Autumn), pp. 5–26.

Asmus, Ronald D., and Robert C. Nurick. 1996. "NATO Enlargement and the Baltic States". *Survival*, Vol. 38, No. 2 (Summer), pp. 121–142.

Bailes, Alyson. 1997. "Europe's Defense Challenge". *Foreign Affairs*, Vol. 76, No. 1 (January/ Feburary), pp. 15–20.

Brown, Michael E. 1995. "The Flawed Logic of NATO Expansion". *Survival*, Vol. 37, No. 1 (Spring), pp. 34–52.

Buzan, Barry. 1991. *People, States and Fear: An Agenda for International Security Studies in the Post-Cold War Era*, 2nd ed. New York: Harvester Wheatsheaf.

Bull, Hedley. 1977. *The Anarchical Society: A Study of Order in World Politics*. New York: Columbia University Press.

Buzan, Barry, Charles Jones, and Richard Little. 1993. *The Logic of Anarchy: Neorealism to Structural Realism*. New York: Columbia University Press.

Clinton, William. 1996. Detroit, Michigan speech, 22 October, reprinted in *The New York Times*, 23 October 1996.

Estonian Review. 1996. Tallinn.

Friedman, Thomas L. 1996. "Help Wanted: Bulldozers". *The New York Times*, 23 October 1996, p. A19.

Heurlin, Bertel. 1996. *Security Problems in the New Europe*. Copenhagen: Copenhagen Political Studies Press.

Holmes, Kim R., and Thomas G. Moore, eds. 1996. *Restoring American Leadership: A U.S. Foreign and Defense Policy Blueprint.* Washington, DC: The Heritage Foundation.

Komsomolskaia pravda. Moscow.

Keohane, Robert O., and Joseph S. Nye. 1977. *Power and Interdependence* (Boston: Little, Brown).

Kionka, Riina, and Raivo Vetik. 1996. "Estonia and the Estonians". In Graham Smith, ed., *The Nationalities Question in the Post-Soviet States*, 2nd ed. London: Longman.

Kirch, Marika, and Aksel Kirch. 1995. "Ethnic Relations: Estonians and Non-Estonians". *Nationalities Papers* Vol. 23, No. 1 (Spring), pp. 43–60.

Krasner, Stephen D. 1982. "Structural Causes and Regime Consequences: Regimes as Intervening Variables," *International Organization*, Vol. 36, No. 2 (Spring), pp. 185–206.

Monitor. Daily report of Jamestown Foundation, Virginia.

Morgenthau, Han. 1967. *Politics Among Nations*, 4th ed. New York: Knopf.

Mueller, John. 1989. *Retreat from Doomsday: The Obsolescence of Major War.* New York: Basic Books.

OMRI Daily Report. Open Media Research Institute Daily Report: Part II – Eastern and Central Europe. Prague.

Perry, William J. 1996. *Annual Report to the President and the Congress.* Washington, DC: U.S. Government Printing Office.

Rossiiskie vesti. Moscow.

United States Department of State. 1996. *Baltic States: USG Policy.* Office of Nordic and Baltic Affairs.

Waltz, Kenneth. 1979. *Theory of International Politics.* Reading, Mass.: Addison-Wesley.

Wendt, Alexander. 1992. "Anarchy is What States Make of It: The Social Construction of Power Politics," *International Organization* 46, No. 2 (Spring), pp. 391–425.

White House. 1995. *A National Security Strategy of Engagement and Enlargement.* Washington, DC: U.S. Government Printing Office.

Chapter 4

NATO, Security, and the Baltic States
A new world, a new security, a new NATO

Bertel Heurlin

Introduction

The new World Order, manifested by a transformation in the organisation of the international system from a two superpower system into an 'only' one superpower system, implies an entirely new security environment for the Baltic States, which during fifty years were Soviet republics. To begin with, the Baltic States regained the sovereignty they lost in 1940. As a follow-up, their surrounding security environment underwent a considerable transformation: Europe, with the disappearance of the iron curtain dividing line, became one coherent continent; the former giant superpower, the Soviet Union, was dissolved; and a new state, Russia, emerged, not as a global power under the flag of dictatorship, but as a regional power adhering to the new global norms of individual freedom, human rights, market economy and democracy. Meanwhile, Germany became united, Poland regained its full sovereignty and autonomy, and Belorussia became an independent state. As an encore, the United States now commands a security overlay covering not just the western part – but the whole of Europe. Subsequently, in becoming a European power, the US can be safely recognised as a Baltic power as well.

Presenting these series of events as a point of departure, it is the aim of this chapter to claim and demonstrate:

- that the Baltic States have never before been positioned in a political-strategic-military environment as secure as the present;
- that this situation is likely to endure;
- that due to the new organisation of the world, the concept of security has changed;

- that NATO is at the point of taking over the Baltic Sea area and transforming it into a 'NATO-lake'.

It is necessary to stress that these theses are entirely dependent upon variations in the positions, capabilities and roles of Russia and the United States.

Portions of this chapter will investigate and present an assessment of the following:

- the Baltic States' security case and dimension, including the strategy, policy, position and international consequences of the Baltic States vis-à-vis NATO;
- the Russian case and dimension as concerns the Baltic States and NATO, outlining its strategy, policy, position and international consequences;
- and finally, the US case and dimension, involving strategy, policy, position and international consequences as well.

The crucial problems being part of the present analysis are the following:

1 Under the present international structure, small states must work hard to be placed high on the superpower's agenda in order to be included as much as possible in the shadow of the American security umbrella. Since the amount of small independent powers in Europe has doubled since the end of the Cold War, freewheeling is no longer an option;
2 Russia – in a spectacular way – is attempting to stop or reduce the NATO enlargement;
3 As the lone superpower, the United States can set the international security agenda and, thus, be at liberty to neglect security problems in Europe – and certainly in the Baltic Sea.

The chapter will consist of the following parts:

- The new security concept and agenda
- The 'new' NATO and NATO expansion
- NATO in the Baltic Sea region
- The Baltic States and NATO
- Russia, NATO and the Baltic States
- Explanation and Conclusion

The new security concept and security agenda

The security agenda in Europe has changed considerably since the end of the Cold War. During the Cold War, security in Europe was indivisible (Heurlin, 1995). In strategic terms, this implied that individual, societal, national, regional and global security was subordinate to international security, in a way where the two superpowers – constituting the 'poles' and the manifestation of world-wide polarisation – left no room in Europe for regional or other conflicts which could affect its division, i.e., a divided Europe presupposed an undivided security. It was a frozen zero-sum situation, different from the Third World where superpower dividing lines were constantly contested and challenged. Due to the concept of 'equal security', which combined the strategy of nuclear stalemate with the notion of a 'seamless web', the dividing line in Europe was sacred. The seamless web indicated the closest connection between the use of the simplest conventional weapons and the use of tactical and strategic nuclear weapons (at least 10,000 such weapons were deployed in the European Theatre). Regional conflicts like Northern Ireland or the Soviet interventions in its European Empire were accepted because they did not "rock the boat".

Today the security agenda has completely changed. With the United States acting as the lone superpower within a unipolar international system, the concept of equal security has never gained full acceptance while the alternative concept of 'common security' has become obsolete. The collective security invented after World War I – and reintroduced in a new manner after World War II – never functioned. In the new world order, however, it proved a fit. In order for collective security to function, it is both necessary to identify 'rogue states', and have them become generally accepted as such by the international society. This presupposes a unipole system. The Gulf War and its aftermath demonstrated the concept of "all against the outcast, the international lawbreaker". The NATO- and UN-supported Bosnia intervention is partly in agreement with the collective security, though no threat to international security was identified as such.

The 'concert-security' model of the 19th century has also been applied after the Cold War to the new security situation. The contact group for ex-Yugoslavia, consisting of the United States, Russia, Germany, France and the United Kingdom, functioned as an informal group of equals i.e., like great powers leaving the other states outside.

However, there is no doubt who the undisputed superior power is: US influence – whether activated or dormant – is overwhelming. With the United States as the leader of Europe, the concert model is only a label with no real content.

'Comprehensive security' was very much on the agenda in the 1970's. Both the United States and the Soviet Union highlighted non-bipolar aspects of security in dichotomies such as rich-poor, producer-consumer, developed-underdeveloped and global dangers as pollution, soil exhaustion, exploitation of the resources, etc. During the second Cold War (79–85), the basic security agenda again focused on international peace and security. Today, with the disappearance of the Cold War the security agenda has expanded even further than during détente. Labelled "soft security", the main issues aside from under-development, famine, catastrophes, and pollution are now refugees, international crime and lack of human rights. The result is that in the absence of military threat – for those not living in the "hot spots" or the European "Islands of conflict" (which we will return to) – individual security, societal security and global security are the areas high on the political agenda. This notion can be characterised as "soft security becoming hard" i.e., as national security (affiliated with military means) is temporarily solved, one must necessarily politicise what really matters: the soft security.

How, then, can the notion of a divided security – and the return of a soft security now considered hard – be applied to the Baltic States? Firstly, it must be stressed that the comprehensive security agenda is certainly operating as part of the present situation in the Baltic Sea region. Interdependence – with its connecting as well as demarcating effects – is a force at play here. The notion of "co-operative security" can also be considered a proper characterisation. Co-operative security refers to a situation where co-operation is the dominant relationship between international actors, and where the potential for military threats is reduced to a very small probability. Both co-operative and comprehensive security will play a crucial role during unipolarity.

But how do these security agendas affect the situation in the Baltic Sea? For the Baltics, the divisibility of security can be assessed as an extremely negative situation. It can imply inclusion into what Russia is now labelling "the near abroad" i.e., the sphere of influence as a legacy from the Soviet Union. Worst case scenario for the Baltic countries is that they will be left as an "island of conflict" or "strategic ghetto", on a par with territories characterised either by the lack of any great power strategic interests (the ex-Yugoslavia area), or by the dominating great power in the area taking matters into its own hands (Northern Ireland or the Caucasus area). This second case looks like it could not be excluded as a possible scenario for the Baltic States.

However, according to present structural conditions, this situation would not be valid for the Baltic States. They will neither become "islands of conflict" nor victims of Russian unilateralism simply because they are not considered inferior cases by the United States i.e., vis-à-vis Russia, these countries rank rather high on the American political agenda. While theoretically, a mutual crisis or clash between one of the Baltic States on the one side and, say, Lithuania and Poland on the other, could easily be positioned in the category of "island of conflict", not so, however, with Russia involved.

The comprehensive security issues – with soft security depending on structural conditions – will be subject to regionalization. Though theoretically global, soft security in practice is not normally maintained on an international, high policy level but rather on a mostly regional level.

Of particular interest to the Baltic States – as well as to all the newly independent states in Europe – is the individual security level. In the new, liberated societies, individual freedom also implies insecurity. Put another way, individual freedom-democratic-free-market-human rights societies can generally be characterised as "risk societies". According to the fundamental norms of the modern risk society, one could make the claim that security is negative while insecurity is positive. Absolute security – in political and economic terms – is tantamount to stagnation, immobility and suppression. This notion refers to the fact that in voting in a democratic society, a political man can never be sure which government will emerge from the election. The experience of ever-changing governments is due to the tyranny of numerous small decisions of the risk society – and the result is insecurity. On the other hand in the risk society you as an individual seldom become subjected to suppression by state authorities normally associated with autocratic and dictatorial regimes.

In the case of economics, insecurity is simply the crucial factor. No economic markets exist without insecurity. Stated another way, insecurity makes the economic world go round. Likewise for the economic man, he will be part of the tyranny of small decisions due to his purchases and investments i.e., the virtue of insecurity.

Recognising this very fact of life in a free (risk) society – along with the influence it can exert on the general public agenda for security – is normally a difficult process precisely because it identifies as a security factor the necessary insecurity for the society and the individual.

In the case of the Baltic countries, this fact is especially crucial. Over the long run, economic insecurity is regulated by a civic society, freedom and the rule of law. The same holds true for the political-democratic insecurity arena. Political and economic insecurity can exist only in a stable, civil society. Consequently as regards the Baltic States, the coming processes vis-à-vis Russia will not only be influenced by national, regional and international security, but certainly by societal and individual security as well.

In sum, the Baltic States have never been more secure in terms of their national security. Under the multipolarity which lasted until the end of World War II, the Baltic States were constantly subjected to the shifting alliances between the poles i.e., the great powers of Europe, the United States, Russia and Japan, and victims of their policies. In this environment, the small states suffered. Denmark, for instance, attempted to forge an alliance with Great Britain but was forced to enter into a non-aggression pact with Germany; subsequently it was occupied. The new Baltic States could not find any protection from among the great powers and, moreover, realised a small power alliance carried no value. Consequently, the German-Soviet agreement of 1939, as well as the subsequent war between them, proved catastrophic for the Baltic States: they were not only dissolved as states, but attempts to destroy them as nations came fairly close to succeeding.

Unipolarity, therefore, seems to be the best of all worlds for small states – the best as long as you are high on the agenda of the world society, or more exactly, of the unipole, the United States. Unipolarity also involves the inclusion of a broader, transnational security concept which invites regionalization and integration, but also can make the individual societies more vulnerable. The same holds true when the modern risk society sets certain limits and conditions on personal security.

The new NATO and NATO expansion

Let us now take a closer look at the national, regional and international security arena, along with the blanketing organisation – NATO. NATO is regionally based and defined. NATO takes its point of departure in the national security of its individual members. NATO functions as a vehicle which attempts to pool the national security issues and strategies of all the memberstates. Regarding international security, NATO is both the strongest *and* longest on-going military alliance based on comprehensive integration ever. Furthermore, in its self-understanding NATO is based on the aims and goals of the United Nations, which is explicitly referred to in the Washington Treaty of 1949.

The end of the Cold War brought on the dissolution of the Warsaw pact. NATO remained however – presumably stronger than ever. On the basis of either historical experience or theoretical considerations, experts and students of international politics predicted that NATO, prolonged for bureaucratic reasons by inventing (more or less) non-convincing new missions, would disappear. It did not – and probably will not – happen. *Why?* To take it one step further, *why even have a NATO when it is generally recognised that there are no major military threats against any of the NATO members?*

The theoretical concept of "international balance of power" as the dominant factor is playing a different role under unipolarity except for local balances-of-power. As long as the United States occupies an unrivalled position in terms of combined capabilities vis-à-vis any other unit or group of units – as is presently the case – the unipolar situation will continue to endure. As we can see in relations between the United States and the European Union, there will certainly be balancing effects on economic capabilities. Even though trade wars are possible, the EU countries – and practically all other states – in terms of security policy are nevertheless "flocking" around the United States; clearly, they are not practising "balancing".

Thus, we have a continuation of the transatlantic alliance in Europe. Due to the disappearance of direct military threats, the tendency is towards weaker and softer alliances (Steven Walt, 1996). Furthermore, there is a tendency – for structural reasons – towards regionalization, with all of Europe now constituting a region, and the Baltic Sea area comprising a subregion.

As the new European power under unipolarity, the United States, together with Europe, is left with the problem of how to cope with this state of affairs; taking centre stage as the most effective and evident factor to solve the security problems is NATO. Among its virtues are: that as an organisation it still thrives; as an alliance it has successfully exceeded its Cold War missions; and to date it continues to be flexible yet stable with the most comprehensive experience in military integration. The most crucial virtue, however, is that it combines Europe with the United States in a most military-integrative way (an integration which will be extended in the direction of supranationalism if a warlike situation occurs). Political in nature, NATO is, however, operating primarily as a military organization. As the European NATO countries have broadly accepted the United States as the provider of security in Europe, this "modus operandi" of NATO stands as a virtue in that it allows the United States to play the undisputed role of leader of the alliance.

In essence, NATO has adapted to the structural, international transformations of the new environment. Fundamentally, NATO is a new organisation which has been careful not to develop into a 'double' organisation – part American and independently, part European . This was was foreseen by some analysts and scholars (e.g. Heurlin,1990). NATO has remained united in one of its main purposes: to manifest the fundamental military and security policy-related link over the Atlantic.

What has changed is the mission as the USSR or Russia is no longer the threat it once was. The chief threat is now Europe's chaotic and unstable past i.e., the possibility of fragmentation, the return to an unstable balance of power situation, or to the reliance on nationalism and hypernationalism. Furthermore, the rogue states represent a threat in that they deliberately subvert attempts to support the new world order because they view the global values of democracy, human rights, individual freedom, and free-market economies as being identical with Western values.

Although NATO has changed its strategy, the military guarantee and "collective defence" notion are still at work. However, they have no value in the present situation: military guarantee, collective defence, flexible response and forward defence are now outdated (though they may return in the distant future). The concept today is one of partnership, conflict management and containment of "islands of conflict". The goal is to integrate all of Europe militarily – particularly Russia. This noble aim is the reason behind the suggestions or establishment of an impressive number of new institutions and organisations closely associated with NATO e.g., NACC, Partnership for Peace, "Superpartnership for Peace" (PfP-Plus), "In the sprit of PfP", The EAPC, The Euro-Atlantic Partnership Council, etc. Each has – or will have – a specific role to play.

Lord Ismay, the first Secretary General of NATO, is said to have coined the simple shorthand for NATO's mission: "to keep the Russians out, the Americans in and the Germans down". Today's revised shorthand could read: "to keep the Americans and Russians in, and Germany and the new members down". "In" refers to the fact that Russia, along with the United States, regard themselves as European powers, in addition to the fact that the US recognises that over the long run, stability in Europe can not be possible without Russia's close co-operation with NATO. "Down" refers to the notion that to become members of NATO on a par with all other NATO states, Germany, together with the East and Central European States, will be subject to a broad-scale military integration which will hinder hypernationalization or the renationalization of the armed forces of the individual countries.

But NATO also has another role to play: it acts as the fundamental factor for establishing and maintain security order in Europe. It is the only organisation that involves the United States directly in vital European affairs; subsequently, the aim is military security. By guaranteeing military security primarily by putting up the umbrella of US protection, NATO is an organisation which will leave room for the Western European countries to maintain, develop and further integration projects on economic and low- or middle-range policy areas. This arrangement may be assessed as an elegant solution to US, Western, and later on Central and Eastern European co-operation. The United States recognises the need for a stable and secure Europe. Subsequently, they take the lead on matters of hard security concerns while the Europeans tend to more soft security matters in areas spelled out in the three pillar structure of the Maastricht treaty, namely: the supranational community issues; the presently very low-profile role of common foreign and security policy issues; and the legal and internal affairs issues.

Constructed in this format, both parties seem to have the best of all worlds: the US can promote European integration – except in the high politics areas where in the final analysis, the *goal is to* secure European stability; and Europe can achieve the gains from the absence of a zero sum game that concerns high political and hard security, enjoy the virtues of economic and technological integration as concerns soft security, and also be allowed to develop a European Security and Defence Identity (ESDI). However, the United States draws the line in that it will not tolerate a common, single, European policy which is detrimental to the US position on issues of vital importance.

In sum, the main purposes and implications of the new NATO in the new Europe are:

- to minimise instability *inside* its area primarily through the military integration including command structures and military multinationalism, implying close co-operation between the individual national military forces; and

- to minimise instability *outside* its area through partnership arrangements and by functioning as a magnet and centre of stability which produces security beyond its membership borders.

In addition, with the current absence of military threats and, consequently, front-line-states or exposed flanks, NATO has the function of preventing security "free-riding" in the sense that the individual member states must become more directly responsible for their own positions in the regional and international system. They all must seek ways to increase their contributions to the security of the alliance rather than just consider how they can profit from the protection of the alliance. Simply put: they must all become producers of security rather than consumers.

If successful, the European member states will also be helping not only to impede the exhaustion of the United States' capabilities, but the possible long-term re-establishment of new "poles" or new aspiring superpowers as well.

The Baltic sea area, the Baltic States and NATO

So, how does this situation affect the Baltic Sea area and the Baltic States? The answer: in the most direct way – perhaps even more than other regions or areas in Europe. During the Cold War, NATO played a less dominating role in Central Europe. There are two main reasons for this: first, there was a plea among Nordic states for the maintenance of what was referred to as "the low tensions of the Nordic states" in not being subjected to the same direct superpower confrontation as in Central Europe. Consequently, the concentration of military presence was less pronounced; second, the notion of the so-called "Nordic Balance" was constructed – with the differing positions of the Nordic States in the Cold War spectre. Finland was the eastward-bound neutral state, Sweden the westward-bound neutral state, and Denmark and Norway – with their fundamental differing geo-strategic positions – were pursuing the same non-provocative approach towards the Soviet Union by emphasising no-nuclear weapons in peacetime and no stationing of foreign troops, and other self-imposed restrictions on military presence in areas close to the Soviet Union (e.g., northern Norway and Bornholm). The claim was that the concept functioned when changes in one end of the politico-military balance would affect changes at the other end. Soviet pressure on Finland, for example, would automatically evoke a reaction in Norway and Denmark – in the direction of closer ties to NATO i.e., by giving up part of their self-imposed restrictions. The notion was used as a political tool by some countries, but inconvenient for others. It was certainly not an analytical concept.

This notion of a Nordic Balance has been reintroduced by some analysts in the 90's as a way to better understand the Baltic Sea situation. In the present analysis of the Baltic Sea area, the Nordic Balance concept certainly seems incorrect and not able to explain or predict the development in the region.

The allegation is that during the Cold War, NATO played a visibly minor role in the Baltic Sea area; in addition, today that role has dramatically changed: NATO is visible, active and determining. Sweden and Finland have joined the PfP and are also observers in the WEU, an organisation which now more than ever is considered the European pillar of NATO. Additionally, Sweden and Finland have suggested at the IGC of the European Union that an enhanced role for the WEU concerning humanitarian and other conflict-managing operations be considered. Poland is expected to be among the new member states included in the alliance in 1999. The new, unified Germany is now *after* 1994 when all Russian troops had left, NATO all over. And Russia, though considering the extension or widening of NATO to be a "serious mistake", has accepted a part in a new NATO-Russian charter i.e., to be included in certain NATO decisions. Russia has accepted operating under NATO command in Bosnia and has also become a member of PfP, though not an very active one. Finally, Russia has set forth bilateral military agreements with NATO countries (e.g. Denmark).

Although the Baltic countries will not be accepted as NATO members in the first round of Central- and Eastern European countries, they will presumably be offered closer relations to NATO through PfP, in a way where Baltic States officers can work closely together with NATO headquarters in an effort to enhance the participation in NATO-organised and led peacekeeping or peace-enforcing operations. Furthermore, the United States – together with the Baltic States – is working out a 'Baltic Action plan' intended to form the basis for a Baltic Charter which could include some implementation of the US-formulated "The door will remain open" concerning Baltic membership. Additionally, the Baltic States have bilateral military agreements with individual NATO countries such as

Denmark, and with PfP countries such as Finland and Sweden. Many bilateral and multilateral military activities and operations are conducted "in the spirit of Partnership for Peace".

Hence, the crucial questions concerning the role of NATO in connection to the Baltic States, and the Baltic States in connection with NATO, are the following:

1 Although Russia is officially reducing its perception that inclusion of the Baltic States would be tantamount not only to a serious provocation, but to a military threat, there remains little doubt that it will react strongly if one or more Baltic states becomes a member of NATO. *How can this position be assessed – especially in terms of a NATO-Russia partnership?*

2 *What role will the European Union play in projecting stability and security to the Baltic States?*

3 The United States has committed itself to a closer military co-operation with the Baltic States primarily through NATO and NATO-centred organisations. *Given that NATO will change in the direction of what is labelled "the new NATO", how will this policy develop? Will NATO become weaker, looser and softer so that widening will imply the opposite of deepening? How to assess military integration and military guarantee? Will the new core functions of NATO move the focus away from article five?*

4 *What will be the role of the new small states – especially the Baltic States – in the new security environment of Europe?*

Russia, NATO and the Baltic States

Russia is the crucial player in the new European security game. On the one hand, all NATO countries will emphasise the agreed policy statement: no lasting security model or architecture without Russia i.e., no new dividing lines in Europe, no more Yaltas. Relations with Russia must be based on partnership.

On the other hand, the core of this policy is also: Russia has a say, but certainly no veto power as concerns the security model. While there are no present threats from Russia, nevertheless, as NATO is open to new members given they fulfil certain conditions, one cannot deny the Central- and Eastern European countries the right to enjoy the same collective security guarantee as present NATO members. *But can Russia apply for NATO-membership? And if not, how is this compatible with the notion of no new border-lines in Europe?*

There are some important observations to be made here. First of all, the security guarantee has to be put in the right perspective. NATO is a collective defence organisation implying that an attack on one member will be regarded as an attack on all member states. However, according to article five, the members are free to select the kind of response they believe should be taken (cit). Secondly, the loose, weak security guarantee has, at least in theory, mostly to do with the threat against the European NATO members. Nobody is forecasting assistance from Euro-NATO in the event of a neighbour-attack on the US. The only possibility here would be a theoretical attack from a more distant, aggressive and aspiring superpower.

In Europe, much depends on Russia and on how NATO chooses to pursue its policy towards Russia. Now let us briefly address Russia's international position after the Cold War. Of course during the Cold War Russia was a superpower. The United States and Russia fought and competed for influence in the world. In Europe, however, the dividing line between East and West was fixed and could not be moved. Here we had a "virtual world war" based mostly on introductions of new weapon systems. In the Third World a continual "proxy war" ravaged. However, the superpowers always avoided any direct military clashes. In the mid-80's, the Soviet Union realised that its policy of protecting its empire by closing it off against the influence of the liberal-capitalist world represented not only by the United States, but also by the Western Countries and the NIC – the newly industrialised countries – was to the detriment to its long-term interests. Gorbachev's strategy of opening up the USSR was an effort to secure its survival and even revive its empire. The tactics would be an accommodation with the West i.e., to "deprive the West the enemy". The Soviet state and its society had been exhausted – economically, politically and militarily – by all the time it had spent standing up to the United States as an equal competitor and opponent.

Of course, the well-documented outcome of the opening up of the Soviet Union and its empire revealed a colossus with feet of clay not able to survive under the new circumstances. Subsequently, a series of developments transpired to weaken and, in the final analysis, dissolve the Soviet Union, none in the slightest way initiated by – or supported by – the West or the United States. The Soviet Union clearly and voluntarily relinquished its role as a superpower and in the end, dissolved itself. In a process directed against the Soviet Union, Russia was re-created as an independent state. It was re-established as a state and a nation which supported – in fact copied – the new global values of the West such as multi-party democracy, individual freedom, human rights and a free-market economy. There was certainly no pressure from the West in this regard. Russia was merely imitating the units of the international system which had succeeded on all levels. Thus, in a way, it is proper to characterise Russia as an Anti-Soviet Union, though according to international law it is legally recognised as the successor state of the USSR

In many ways, Russia is not the USSR. It is not a superpower. Rather, it is a medium regional power with combined capabilities far below the United States and far below units such as China, Japan and insofar as it can be considered an independent international unit, the European Union.

Any comparison with Russia to Germany after World War I and II (Versailles-Yalta-Potsdam) is misleading. In addition, there are remarkable differences between the dissolution of the Soviet empire and the dissolution of other empires like the French or the British. The Soviet empire was dissolved in three phases: first, the Third World portion of the empire was given up; second, the Eastern European; and third, the Soviet Union itself. In this last phase, Russia disassociated itself from the content of this unit. This was certainly not the case for France or the UK. If any comparison can be hinted at, the dissolution of the Ottoman empire would be the choice: the secular, modern Turkey of Kemal Atatürk was established as a deliberate anti-Ottoman empire. The idea of the new Russian state embodied a modern, open, democratic, market economy-oriented civic society, the identity and roots of which being those of pre-Revolutionary Russia. The project incorporates Anti-Soviet Union features as well.

The success of this transformation is of course difficult to accept for great parts of the Russian population. Even more crucial is the acknowledged reduced role and position of Russia in regional and World Affairs. In political, economic and military terms, Russia is quite another unit than the Soviet Union. It will no doubt be a painful process for Russia to realise the new regional and international rules of the game. And two of the most pertinent problems in this game are precisely the expansion of NATO and the position of the Baltic States.

Perhaps as a sign of things to come, the March 1997 Helsinki Summit showed Russia's broad understanding of the transformed conditions in the international system. Russia seems to have realised that its interests are best managed by 'flocking around' the lone superpower – the United States – rather than balancing against it. Stressing its negative attitude toward the expansion project, Russia nevertheless accepted an agreement which brought it closer to the NATO organisation. Additionally, Yeltsin's declaration of willingness and preparedness to join the European Union signified the fundamental Russian interest in a drive towards the new centre in Europe, and a drive towards the West in general. With the formulation of the NATO-Russia charter, Russia has not only signalled that NATO – with the United States as undisputed leader – can play a significant role in maintaining security in Europe, but that it is compatible with fundamental Russian interests as well.

How, then, can we identify Russian national interests and how is Russia coping with the interests of NATO as an organisation? Theoretically, Russia has interests similar to any other nation in the international system: to maintain and secure Russia's existence, sovereignty, autonomy, integrity and identity, material status and a benign and non-threatening environment. Basically, Russia's problems lie in its existence: *Will it be able to exist as a federation consisting of 89 entities – or will it dissolve?* NATO's position has been to support the existence of Russia as is. This also goes for sovereignty and autonomy. The integrity goal is somewhat problematic, however. It involves the fact that 25% of the Russian population is living outside the borders of the federation. In the Baltic countries, this amount is more than 1.3 million. In Latvia, approximately 800,000 Russians are living as a stateless class because of the great difficulty in obtaining Latvian statehood. Russia is using these conditions as a constant pressure and an open possibility for interfering in Baltic internal affairs. The goal of material status is strong and significant: in order to enhance its position, Russia sees its interest in maintaining the best possible relations with the West because it realises that in economic terms, opening towards the West is, in the long run, a prerequisite if not for survival, then at least for stability and prosperity.

With regard to its geo-political environment, Russia is in a complex situation as to how to relate to the new organisation of Europe and how to exert influence on the regional and international system. Four layers can be identified:

First, the former enemies from bipolarity i.e., in broad terms, the Western European Countries and America.

Here partnership is the notion, but still there are reminiscences of mutual distrust.

Second, the former satellites in Central and Eastern Europe who, during the Cold War, had lost their independence.

Now fully independent states, they will pursue a policy towards Russia – independent of the fact that Russia is not the USSR – taking into consideration that "the past is not going to happen again". Their applications to join NATO must be assessed on this basis.

Third, the former Soviet Republics *forced into the Union, considering their relations to the Soviet Union form 1940–91 as pure occupation.*

These are the three Baltic States. Due to the occupation conception, they will have a particular and complicated relation to Russia for a rather long time. Their application to join NATO, along with their close relations to NATO through PfP and the bilateral and multi-lateral military activities in the spirit of PfP relative to NATO member countries has not eased the situation.

The Baltic States are worried that because of their unpredictable, large neighbour, their security situation is fragile. Russia is emphasising that it has been betrayed by the Western powers because it i.e., in the shape of the Soviet Union, voluntarily rolled back its empire and reduced itself on the basis of a vision of a Europe free of competitive military alliances. And the result seems to be directly the opposite: under NATO, the western military alliance is constantly coming closer and, in the final analysis, incorporating the Baltic countries, former Soviet territories and even territories also occupied by former Soviet military bases and installations.

It must be stressed, however, that it is unlikely that the Baltic States will accept any restrictions in their foreign policy goals as concerns sovereignty, autonomy or integrity, and especially in terms of any notion of "Russian spheres of influence" or "near abroad-ism". On the other hand, it is in the best interests of the Baltic States to come to terms with their large neighbour and accept a policy which will demand hard work while still seeking to be as close to the military-political centre, the NATO and economic centre, and the European Union as possible.

Because Russia voluntarily provided for the above transformations, it basically must accept the completely new circumstances in the Baltic Sea. By declaring itself a sovereign federation in 1991, Russia also brought about the full freedom and sovereignty of the Baltic States. It must be re-emphasised that no outside pressure was directed against either the Soviet Union or Russia. Hence, Russia must take the consequences of its own policy.

Fourth, the former Soviet Republics which now are organised in the Commonwealth of Independent States (CIS).

Though they all have close relations to Russia, their dependence differs and is, in fact, increasing. Most of the CIS states are indifferent or negative to NATO expansion. However, positive statements from the Ukraine in early 1997 may indicate a coming general acceptance. The Ukraine is striving to be treated at the same level as NATO is treating or negotiating with Russia. The CIS states are all members of NACC and most of them are actively participating in Partnership for Peace. Presumably, they will all become members of the Euro-Atlantic Partnership Council to be established in mid-1997.

Within each of these four layers, NATO plays a different role and, subsequently, has a varying standing and impact upon the security situation. But all in all, NATO has taken over the drawing table for the new security architecture in Europe. The crucial problem, however, is Russia itself.

Under an analytical lens, it appears that the security situation for Russia, using unipolarity as point of departure, looks like the following: Russia is in no way threatened by NATO because NATO is the only operative and efficient organisation which can take care of the security in Europe. Additionally, Russia is striving for an effective partner relationship with the leader of NATO, the United States. Russia sees no need for counterbalancing the US because there seems to be no evidence of allies aligned with such a move, and they realise that there are more gains than losses to be obtained from 'flocking around the US'.

In a certain sense, the United States is also preoccupied with assisting the enhancement of Russian security. Curiously enough, one way is through NATO, with its enlarged mission of taking care of internal security and functioning as a zone of stability and integration. Alternatives to NATO enlargement could be one of three possibilities:

1 Hypernationalism or Re-hypernationalism in the Central- and Eastern European states. With independent, chauvinistic, arms race-infected armed forces, this would be contrary to military forces integrated in NATO command structures and other integrative structures which would better serve Russian national interests.

2 The formation of an independent military alliance of former Warsaw Pact countries with the purpose of avoiding a repetition of the late 40's Russia – where countries were taken over based upon the later formulated Brezhnev Doctrine.

3 The formation of interwar period-like military alliances between the individual Central and Eastern European countries and the greater powers of Western Europe e.g., Germany (in combination with, say, Poland and/or Hungary), France (with Rumania and/or the Czech republic), the United Kingdom (with the Baltic countries), etc. This would leave the core of Europe in an organisational mess security policy-wise, and cause an instability that would be considered negative for Russian interests.

According to the theory, these considerations would signify that Russia, at least over the long run, would be willing to accommodate NATO in both its taking over of European security, and in its enlargement.

Conclusions

It was originally stated at the beginning of this chapter that what we now have is a new NATO in a new Europe. Furthermore, it was emphasised that the virtues of NATO are, primarily, that it is a military organisation promoting peace through military integration and that it is relying entirely on the leading position of the United States. This is consistent with the fact that the European Union is a political-economic institution maintaining and promoting peace through economic and political integration.

The evident conclusions for this chapter are: that NATO has taken over the security of all of Europe, and that long term development will diminish the distinction between NATO commitments directly related to article five and those that are not. It is the claim here that new and expanded institutions such as the Partnership for Peace will function as the effective "eraser" of possible new boundaries in Europe. The idea is that as NATO expands, PfP will take up a renewed attempt to erase new borderlines.

In addition, the chapter demonstrated that security under the new structural organisation of the international system – unipolarity – is no longer subject to the indivisibility of security i.e., if there is a lack of overall European-NATO strategic interest in an area of conflict, "islands of conflict" may emerge. The main question would then be: *Precisely where do the Baltic states belong?* Here, there seems to be no divergence of theoretical assessments: with the exception of intra-Baltic small state conflicts, they are geographically, strategically, politically and economically positioned in an area which is covered by the overall broad NATO security umbrella.

This subsequently leads to the basis of the claim that *in terms of security, never before have the Baltic States been in a situation where they could be assessed so secure as in the present environment.* And this situation is presumably not going to disappear over night. Unipolarity, which is the fundamental basis for this assessment, is expected to endure for some time. If and when the international system is again transformed, there will be a warning time.

From time to time the Baltic States are confronted with signals which could be interpreted as somewhat alarming. Due to new centres in Europe, the emerging and expanding European Union, and a transformed and expanding NATO, the Baltic States – though not directly incorporated but merely attached to these centres – are for the present and foreseeable future fairly well-off hard security-wise. In terms of soft security areas, there remains plenty of hard work to be done. The same holds true for the Baltic countries' direct bilateral relations with Russia: they will have to be prepared to highlight their share of contribution to the emerging NATO-European Union security system in Europe.

Literature

Asmus, Ronald D., Richard L. Kugler and F. Stephen Larrabee. 1996. "What Will NATO Enlargement Cost?" *Survival* 38:5–26.

Bailes, Alyson J. K. 1996. "NATO: Towards a New Synthesis." *Survival* 38:27–40.

Bland, Douglas L. 1991. *The Military Committee of the North Atlantic Alliance: A Study of structure and strategy.* New York: Praeger.

Brown, Michael E. 1995. "The flawed logic of NATO expansion." *Survival* 37:34–52.

Carpenter, Ted Galen, ed. 1994. "The future of NATO." A special issue of *The Journal of Strategic Studies* 17:1–169.

Christensen, Thomas J., and Jack Snyder. 1990. "Chain gangs and passed bucks: Predicting alliance patterns in multipolarity." *International Organization* 44:137–68.

Cornish, Paul. 1996. "European security: the end of architecture and the new NATO." *International Affairs* 72:751–769.

DUPI. 1997. *Danish Foreign Policy Yearbook 1997.* Copenhagen, DUPI.

Eyal, Jonathan. 1996. "NATO and European Security." *Perspectives* 6/7:17–27.

Eyal, Jonathan. 1995. "Post-election foreign policy: America's leadership, America's opportunity." *Foreign Policy* 98:6–27.

Eyal, Jonathan. 1994/95. "NATO's functions after the cold war." *Political Science Quarterly* 190:763–87.

Grobel O., Lejins A., eds. 1996. *The Baltic Dimension of European Integration*. Riga: LIIA, IEWS, Royal Danish Embassy, Riga.

Hansen, Birthe (ed.). 1995. *European Security – 2000*. Copenhagen Political Studies Press.

Hansen, Birthe. 1997. *Unipolarity and the Middle East*. (forthcoming).

Hellmann, Gunther, and Reinhard Wolf. 1993. "Neorealism, neoliberal institutionalism, and the future of NATO." *Security Studies* 3:3–43.

Heurlin, Bertel. 1997. "Military Command Structures in the Baltic Sea Area". *NEBI-Yearbook 1997*, (forthcoming).

Heurlin, Bertel. 1990. "NATO, Europa, Danmark." Copenhagen, SNU.

Heurlin, Bertel. 1995. *Security Problems in the New Europe. Six Essays on European, German, Baltic, Nordic and Danish Security*. Copenhagen Political Studies Press.

Heurlin, Bertel. 1996. *The US Impact in European Security as we Approach the Year 2000*. Orrenius, Anders and Truedson, Lars. eds. Olof Palme International Center, Stockholm, pp. 118–135.

Joenniemi, Pertti & Carl-Einar Stålvant (eds.). 1995. *Baltic Sea Politics. Achievements and Challenges*. The Nordic Council.

Knudsen, Olav F. 1996. *Bound to Fail? Regional security cooperation in the Baltic Sea Area and Northeast Asia*. Working Paper, NUPI, Norge.

Krohn, Axel (ed.). 1996. *The Baltic Sea Region. National and International Security Perspectives*. Baden-Baden: Nomos Verl.-Ges.

Kupchan, Charles A., and Clifford A. Kupchan. 1995. "The promise of colllective security." *International Security* 20:52–61.

Lejins A., Bleiere D., eds. 1996. *The Baltic States, Search for Security*. Latvian Institute of International Affairs.

Lejins, Atis. 1996. "The 'Threat' of NATO Enlargement to the Security of the Baltic States." *Kungl Krigsvetenskapsakademiens Handlinger och tidskrift* 200:77–82.

Lepgold, Joseph. 1994. "Does Europe have a place in U.S. foreign policy? A domestic politics argument." In *Discord and collaboration in a new Europe: Essays in honor of Arnold Wolfers*, edited by Douglas T. Stuart and Stephen F. Szabo. Washington, D.C.: Johns Hopkins Foreign Policy Institute.

Lepgold, Joseph. 1995. "Does the United States make sense in NATO after the cold war? On what terms?" In *Post-cold war policy: The international context*, edited by William Crotty. Chicago: Nelson-Hall.

Lähteenmäki, Kaisa (ed.). 1994. *Dimensions of Conflict and Cooperation in the Baltic Sea Rim*. Tampere Peace Research Institute Research Report No. 58.

McCalla, Robert B. 1996. "NATO's persistence after the cold war." *International Organization* 50:445–75.

Mearsheimer, John J. 1990. Back to the future: Instability in Europe after the cold war. *International Security* 15:5–56.

Mearsheimer, John J. 1994/95. "The false promise of international institutions." *International Security* 19:5–49.

Moshes, Arkady & Anton Vushkarnik. 1997. Russia and the Baltic States: Between Coexistence and Cooperation?. *IWPS* 1:77–100.

NATO handbook 1995. Brussels: NATO Information Service.

Nordic Council. 1995. *Towards a Baltic Sea Region*. The Nordic Council.

Nordic Forum for Security Policy. 1997. *St Petersburg, the Baltic Sea and Euroopean Security.* Helsinki: The Finnish Committee for European Security (STETE).

Nye, Joseph S., and William A. Owens. 1996. America's Information Edge. *Foreign Affairs* 75:20–36.

Petersen, Nikolaj (ed.). 1993. *The Baltic States in International Politics.* The Danish Institute of International Studies, DJØF Publishing, Copenhagen.

Ruggie, John Gerard. 1996. Consolidating the European Pillar: The Key to NATO's Future. *The Washington Quarterly* 20:109–124.

Snyder, Glenn H. 1991a. "Alliances, balance, and stability." *International Organization* 45:121–42.

Snyder, Glenn H. 1991b. "Alliance theory: A neorealist first cut." In *The evolution of theory in international relations,* edited by Robert L. Rothstein. Columbia: University of South Carolina Press.

U.S. Department of State. 1997. *Report to the Congress on the Enlargement of the North Atlantic Treaty Organization: Rationale, Benefits, Cost and Implications.*

Walt, Stephen M. 1987. *The origins of alliances.* Ithaca. N.Y.: Cornell University Press.

Waltz, Kenneth N. 1979. *Theory of international politics.* Reading, Mass.: Addison-Wesley.

Weber, Steve. 1992. "Shaping the postwar balance of power: Multilateralism in NATO." *International Organization* 46:633–80.

Chapter 5

The Baltic States and Security Strategies Available

Birthe Hansen

The purpose of this chapter is to summarise the international conditions which the three reborn Baltic States operate within in an attempt to present available security strategy alternatives. The study will focus on the concept of *unipolarity* as the paper aims to analyse the effects specific unipolar political dynamics have upon Baltic security efforts.

During the international transformation process from Cold War to the current world order, the three Baltic states of Estonia, Latvia and Lithuania reclaimed their independence from within a collapsing Soviet empire. This rebirth occurred within a fundamentally altered international environment. Not only had the Baltic States been liberated from their Cold War past, but similar opportunities and necessities to reformulate international ambitions and positions were confronted by the rest of the international system. Within the context of these events, the restructuring of the international system needs to be incorporated into a security analysis of the Baltic States' present situation.

Politically as well as analytically, the Baltics' re-emergence to independent statehood late in the summer of 1991 has attracted substantial attention. As the newcomers' re-emergence necessarily implies a substantial challenge, both to themselves and to the international environment, this attention appears justified. While their internal challenges can neatly be summed in terms of securing and improving their societies and states, challenges to the international system are less simple to state. Hence, in an environment of numerous actors, each with its competing and contrasting objectives, the reverse question of how the Baltic States manage assimilation – or not – is a complex one.

As Estonia, Latvia and Lithuania are all small states, weak in capabilities, they will likely be inclined to adopt the 'world order condition'. Because of relative weaknesses, they can ill afford not to take this condition into consideration. Accordingly, it is clear beyond doubt that the Baltics' efforts will be heavily dependent upon the international environment. Therefore, in order to determine the Baltics' ability to manage contemporary international challenges, an analytical framework dealing with the post-Cold War international dynamics will be applied.

The framework is based on the model for unipolarity (Hansen 1993 and 1995). The model draws heavily on the classic neorealist theory (Waltz 1979) and aims at presenting theoretical statements on the international dynamics in the case of a distribution of power in favour on only one superpower in existence. Empirically the resulting assessement was the identification of the United States being in a position as a single superpower after 1989, and the assessment thus led to the application of the model. Consequently the US has been attributed with the characteristics of a unipole, the combination of its unipolar position and its global strategy is referred to as the US World Order, the dynamics of a unipolar international system are considered to shape the security conditions of all states, and the the security conditions of the small states (i.e., all other states) are analysed in terms of the theoretical statements on unipolarity. Moreover, it is taken well for granted that the dominant tendency of state behaviour after the end of the Cold War will be adaptation to the unipolar order, and that the adaptation will include the strive of the individual states to maximize their own international position (which, of course, comprises no guarantee of success or wisdom). The relevant statements for analysing the security strategies of the Baltics' are put forward below, and the method has been to interpret the strategical options according to the statements.

Hopefully there will be more benefit from the application of the model for unipolarity: In the first place the application aims at bringing about further understanding of the Baltics' security situation, and in the second place the Baltics' case represents an opportunity to explore whether or not the model works in a 'new' case.

Estonia, Latvia and Lithuania are, by no means, brand new states. However, whenever statehood is new or regained, circumstances suggest a series of related problems and challenges, just as profound alterations to the internal structure of an existing state may cause fundamental international redirection. Such was the case with Iran after the Islamist revolution. It is a simple fact that the formation of new states disperses old equilibriums of power, and challenges interstate patterns of conflict and co-operation.

The statehood dimension, however, is only one part of the Baltic challenge. The immense 1989 transformation of the international environment is another dimension which requires skilful handling. Affecting the relations of strength, the creation of new states necessarily alters fundamental international balances of power, and the present dynamics of the balances are no longer linked to the Cold War and the so-called 'zero sum' game of the bipolar superpowers. Rather, while no definitive analytical agreement has been reached, it is herein taken for granted that two features of the 'new' dynamics must include the premises that: a) power still matters and; b) current international distributions of power should be analysed along unipolar lines i.e., the international system as characterised by the existence of only one superpower.

Moreover, specific dynamics, which arguably elicit particular state behaviours (albeit with some limitations according to the specific context of individual states), can be attributed to the condition of unipolarity. Geopolitically, for instance, the Baltics are concerned with the question of alignment and a choice of three alternative strategies: neutrality, close co-operation with Russia, or Western alignment? Since their independence, the Baltic States have clearly formulated decisions favouring of the latter. Therefore, the option of Western alignment will be the primary focus of this analysis.

In order to provide a current (and temporary) view on the question of security, the scope of this analysis will be limited. A temporary view is a prerequisite when attempting to analyse within the context of a transitional phase. It is evident to state that Estonia, Latvia and Lithuania are indeed three different states. Although this analysis does not intend to downplay or neglect their differences, emphasis will focus on the similarities between these comparatively small new-comers.

With these modifications in mind, this chapter, based on post-1989 unipolar international arrangements and by means of the model for unipolarity, will aim to present a security analysis of the Baltic States which takes into account the experiences and decisions of the five-year period. The analysis will be broken down into the following six parts: a) The question of security will be addressed within the context of the analytical framework of this work i.e., a 'neorealist' model for unipolarity; b) Baltic capabilities will be examined, both individually and collectively; c) Regional changes vis-à-vis the actors will be identified; d) External challenges will be identified (with emphasis on the Baltic-Russian relationship); e) Strategic options will be drafted;

and f) Available security strategies (including the option for a 'balanced co-operative security') will be assessed.

The question of security and the theoretical framework

The analytical prerequisite for this chapter is the conceptualisation of a changed security environment, along with the challenges of operating within a unipolar structure. This conceptualisation is based on a unipolar model formulated from the abstract, yet mutually consistent, theoretical statements of international systems characterised by the existence of only one superpower (Hansen 1995). The scope of this model will analyse international politics so as to include the politics of minor states such as the Baltics. State behaviour, consequently, is generally considered to operate within the present *unipolar security condition* which, in general, is characterised by (cf. Hansen 1993 and 1995):

- No 'great power' rivalry
- Less 'great power' pressure as well as support i.e., more hard work with respect to small state co-operation and conflict
- More freedom of action for small states
- Regionalisation (including conflict and co-operation)
- A unique and powerful position for the United States (as a unipole)
- Flocking, i.e., a tendency to rely on the United States in case of hard security problems
- Strong incentives to emulate the winning model of democracy and market economy

As the model claims a general validity, and aims for the inclusion of all states, these conditions[1] are argued to be crucial for the Baltic States and their security efforts, as well as for explanatory attempts with respect to their post-1989 political records.

In terms of other important differences between the Cold War and the current world order, debates have centred around the notion that 'soft security', rather than military issues, have apparently come to dominate the international agenda. Some examples include ecological concerns, minority rights and social issues. Up until the early Nineties, such issues were regarded as 'less important' and local matters, and therefore often given low priority vis-à-vis the overwhelming threats arising from the nuclearised superpower rivalry. Presently, it appears as if soft security matters have indeed replaced harder security issues in dominating the international agenda. Historically, however, the emergence of soft security issues can be seen as a cyclical phenomenon occurring after periods of 'hard security' – and, issues of soft security may also turn 'hard'. Therefore, the notion should be used as a temporary application only; it should not portray an irreversible international process.

As long as indications bode well for stable and clear interstate relations, states, in the absence of great power rivalries, will tend to grant high priority to soft security. In order to lay the groundwork for later needs arising from a harder sphere, states need to attend the capabilities which have been suppressed during times of confrontation. Because they can ill afford to fall short in any capability area, small states need to adapt to the requirements of softer periods of state interaction. As a consequence to cope with the soft agenda is an essential, and even necessary, condition which also represents an opportunity to small states.

In the case of the Baltics (and their limited potentials in coping with a hard security environment), the current situation represents a comparatively favourable climate in which to better the prospects for consolidating statehood, expanding capabilities and increasing their attractiveness to greater powers. Current efforts, if skilfully managed, may subsequently turn into valuable assets in times of deteriorating international climates. The consequence of pursuing a soft agenda must result in the redirection of particular capabilities suited for dealing with such issues as economic performance. Meanwhile, prospects for the long-term re-emergence of harder issues ought not to be neglected. Regardless, it is a necessity during the current soft period (not least for minor states) that energy be spent on building up a wide range of capabilities.

The abovementioned conditions are the result of a fundamental change in the world order, and thus hold implications for all states. A successful adaptation to the present new world order necessarily means that these conditions must be taken into account by all states, including the Baltics. Despite their obvious differences, however, the Baltic States face a major common challenge.

The effects of a changing security framework which includes a disposition towards 'regionalisation' are, in the case of the Baltics, reinforced due to a deficit in their ability to project power of any kind. During the Cold War, the Baltic Sea area was as divided and militarised as the rest of Europe (although the levels of militarisation and tension were comparatively low). Since 1989, however, the situation has become one 'of ease' as the area appears to have become a centre of potential and actual co-operation. Estonia's, Latvia's and Lithuania's renewed independent appearance has increased the number of sovereign states around the Baltic Sea.

Conversely, the littoral boundaries of Russia have substantially been reduced (in comparison to their former Soviet expanse), while Germany's boundaries (owing to unification), have been increased. Furthermore, Poland, freed from the bindings of the former Eastern political empire, has begun *to act* as an independent state.

Consequently, with the transformation from the former regional set-up (which included a number of smaller states and one dominant superpower – which the Baltics were part of) to the present enlarged and more equal set-up (which features the rise of a larger number of competing regional powers), the Baltic Sea area has grown more complicated. Although the overwhelming threat of a bipolar nuclearised rivalry has abated, the implications of this new arrangement bode for an increased number of potential conflicts and alignments. Currently, however, the major regional powers are focusing on other issues: Germany, so far, has abstained from pursuing a dominant role; Russia has redefined its approach to the Baltic area; and Poland is busily preoccupied with its Western relations.

On the other hand, the Baltic area, as the superpower rivalry has lifted (Heurlin 1995), has also become an area more disposed to co-operation (as the obstacles to co-operation and interaction have disappeared). Within the context of a low tension unipolar environment, the complex pursuit of multilateral relations thus appears to be an opportunity rather than a restraint. For the Baltics, this entails a more complex regional environment gaining in importance, as well as a window of opportunity for greater manoeuvrability in their choice of security strategies including the choice of a 'Western alignment'.

As previously alluded to, even the question of 'security' is in dispute today. Conceptualised here, security falls under a theoretical understanding which characterises the international system as being anarchical and competitive by nature. States needing to help themselves in order to care for their relative positions (cf. Waltz 1979) must continuously seek to improve capabilities ranging from internal stability and political competence to economic performance and military strength. Relative gains in aggregate capabilities ultimately means more security (and vice versa). The most effective way to compensate for the lack of certain capabilities is to ally with other states (where possible).

The concept of 'alignment' is a state's strategy for adding capabilities or increasing the value of existing ones. In reality, alignments appear over a wide scale ranging from defence alliances to commitments of a much lesser degree. States always face a dilemma in respect to alignment and its variety of commitments (G. Snyder 1984). Close commitment, labelled as 'chain-gang' (Snyder and Christensen 1990), provide allies with security, but also exposes them to their allies' problems. This strategy can reduce autonomy. A strategy of no commitment, labelled as 'passing the buck' (op.cit.), increases a state's autonomy (see also Morrow 1987), but also exposes it to threats. Small states geographically adjacent to major powers have an additional problem: neither option ensures benefit. Regardless of the chosen strategy, small states may be subject to indirect losses of security and autonomy (Walt 1987). In the case of 'high politics', the major powers are inclined to decide which side their small neighbours fall on. Should the international climate deteriorate i.e., should the balance of power between major powers change, the Baltic States would face a severe political dilemma. At present, as the international environment is stable and encourages 'soft' alignment, they are 'protected'.

Under the present unipolar conditions, the Baltics naturally have an incentive, if threats are perceived, to flock around the one real superpower. In the event Russia were to re-emerge as a true superpower – or even attempt to – the Baltics would face a hard risk of being squeezed. In the meantime, however, the Baltics' alignment efforts should be interpreted as a means of increasing the value of their capabilities (in general), rather than their 'taking sides' in any polarising conflict.

In summary, in the Baltic States' attempt to enhance their respective and collective positions, unipolar incentives, together with their individual capability profiles within a changing international (regional) environment, forces the Baltics to seek co-operation with strategies of soft alignment. Conversely, however, (Western) alignment is not a fully reliable strategy for small states bordering a major power alignments as the Baltics do.

The Baltic States' capabilities

Applying the theoretical considerations to an analysis of the Baltic States' capabilities includes the notion 'strength matters'. This notion is valid even in the face of diminished military threats when states can focus on progress in other dimensions rather than devoting all resources to the task of deterrence. This approach is derived from the 'neorealist' theory (cf. Waltz 1979) and carries seven criteria for measuring strength: a) size of territory; b) size of population; c) economic capability; d) military capability; e) resource endowment; f) political cohesion; and g) political competence.

In terms of population and territorial size, all three Baltic states fare poorly. Estonia's and Latvia's populations total numbers inferior to those of the world's big cities while their territories fare similarly in comparisons. Lithuania has a larger population and greater territory, but on a relative basis, must still be considered a state of a very small scale. None of the three states possess particularly rich endowments of natural resources either. On the world map, the Baltics must be considered 'insignificant' with respect to these parameters, and attempts to increase them will be difficult at best. With the issue of security conceptualised to encompass the relative gains of aggregate capabilities, attention must be directed to the remaining four parameters: economic capability, military strength, political stability and competence.

Economically, the picture of the Baltics is a mixed one. In comparison to the core of the Western community[2], their development toward success in world markets is poor and lacking. They are, however, in a better position than other states of similar circumstance i.e., other new ex-Soviet states. As an example, throughout their Soviet past, the population was comparatively well educated, skilled in industrial functions and specialised in high-level industry. Consequently, people of the Baltic region today are able to consume and produce more relative to their fellow new-states. Therefore, the Baltics possess substantial potential for economic interactions with the West. So far Estonia has proved that. The Estonian economic development has been characterized by speed and adjustment, and it already meets EU standards, and all the Baltic states have progressed in terms of meeting the new demands.

In fact, economic prospects for the Baltics already appear to include benefits from its co-operation with the West: in their position as viable markets (due to comparatively high abilities among new market options for the West to invest in); in their position as industrial sub-producers (due to qualitative steps of Western core countries into positions as post-industrial producers[3]); and in their position within a 'learning' dimension (with the West acting as both a locomotive and helper by institutional means of emulation).

In terms of military capability, historical evidence proves that each Baltic state – or perhaps even the three combined – have been unable to successfully defending themselves vis-à-vis the major powers. Their capability deficit in this regard is an immanent part of their small scale nature. Whether to maintain a low (neutral) profile or seek to join an alliance (with its subsequent costs and benefits) in the hopes of combining weak capabilities is always a dilemma for small states. The dilemma is highlighted by the socalled 'power of the weak', i.e., the option of free-riding, which is, however reduced in the case of unipolarity owing to the hard work condition.

To date, implementation of important decisions are already underway; each has opted in favour of developing their own military force and has seriously signalled their wish to join NATO. Regardless of the outcome, these decisions represent strong signals of will toward self-help and, particularly in the case of NATO, indicate willing profiles well beyond low and neutral. As NATO itself undergoes transformation into a different institution (Heurlin 1990), concerned with expanding the Western spheres, the Baltics' inclinations are to be considered 'soft'. With a territorial position adjacent to the 'new' Russia, the Baltics are guaranteed a special Western attention as they also rim the EU. In light of the international focus on 'soft security', the Baltics are presumably going to assess as superior the benefits of a mutual partnership in the world order *with* Russia in the longer term as opposed to the related dangers of a partnership without Russia.

Political stability and competence are two other capabilities potentially primed for relative expansion. Though both capabilities are sensitive to the present state-building processes taking place in the Baltic region, they are less tied to 'actual size' than the other capabilities. However, political stability, in particular, risks impediment by current state-building processes.

The Soviet Union, in classic 'great power' style, during World War II deliberately tried to change the demographic composition of its peripheral stretch. Therefore, as with other new-born states formerly occupied or part of a fallen great power, the Baltics are today a mixed population. Russians compromise approximately one third of the population of Estonia, more than one third of Latvia and an estimated 8–10% of Lithuania. As such, Estonian and Latvian societies can be characterised as mixed. The size of the Russian minority exposes both the risk for societal instability as well as the potential political problems lying within Baltic-Russian relations. Although parts of the Russian community adhere to Baltic independence, others feel endangered and subject to social regression. This situation creates an inherent danger because the abandonment by Russia has left its citizens within the Baltic region potentially feeling deserted and therefore attracted to, or prone to seek protection from, their former patron-like authorities.

Aside from the minority issue, social problems also represent a challenge to the political stability of the Baltics. The process of 'modernisation', together with the process of internal transformation, tends to bring about internal unrest. The Baltic States have begun implementing substantial internal changes in the desire to transform their economies from a 'planned-model' to a 'free-market' model as rapid privatisation of these former planned economies and the 'breaking away' from the former Soviet Union (today Russia is Latvia's and Lithuania's most important trade partner, and the second of Estonia. Before, of course the Soviet Union was by far the most important commercial partner in the area), and meetings with world markets are all factors having severe impact on the Baltic societies. Conventional wisdom dictates that although these processes will likely command long-term benefits for a majority of the population, 'losers' will be created along the way. One group destined to be losers will undoubtedly be former Soviet staffers (as a recent example in the closing of Soviet factories in Lithuania shows). As a result, they may seek to form alliances with other Balts who can not adapt to the new market conditions; both groups, naturally, would have a predisposition to opposing the new Baltic elites. Though the international environment has, to this point, been attentive and supportive of the situation, it has also made demands. The Baltic states, for their part, have met these demands by facilitating the daily life of the Russian minorities along with their attempts to 'humanise' the transition to a free-market model. Yet internal challenges remain.

With respect to capabilities in political competence, the new Baltic elites have thus far achieved a rather successful record. They have made dramatic decisions concerning military build-up and institutional affiliations; on balance, it seems they have lost little while gaining a great deal. In the process, they have managed to transform their societies without the frequent upheavals such processes dictate. Relative to many other states in transformation (as, for example, in the Middle East), they have been more effective in managing their way. The Russian process is still not an irreversible one, although the unipolar conditions most likely will restrain Russia. The process of transformation is in the making and the development in Russia may yet lead to major and difficult Baltic decisions.

In summary, each of the three Baltic states is characterised by 'smallness'. Although they possess certain potentials, and lack certain capabilities, on balance they remain vulnerable. In Estonia and Latvia, minority issues and the risk of conflict with Russian interests top the agenda. Within all three states, social problems originate from the transformation process. However, within a scenario lacking in any urgent military threats, the Baltics are provided strong incentive to opt for a secure and stable environment (and thus friendly relations with all neighbours) in order to reap the benefits of the substantially increased opportunities under international co-operation.

Regional Changes and the World Order

After 1989 general regional changes, and specifically those in the Baltic Sea area, could be characterised by a strong institutional activity, a reduced attention from the great powers and changes in the number and nature of the units. As discussed above, Estonia, Latvia and Lithuania are prone to make up for their capability shortcomings by means of interstate co-operation and soft alignment. Though regional co-operative efforts, today, are carried out in a completely different context than during the Cold War, they remain no less important. Relations are carried out with a number of other states (and groups of states) who are also attempting to adapt to the unipolar world order, as well as with each other.

With respect to the Baltics' relationship to their regional surroundings, the post-Cold War political landscape includes the following actors:

a) *Russia*, which is in the process of reconstruction and nation-building after the dissolution of the Soviet Empire;
b) *The United States*, which is currently the only superpower in existence (and superior to regional borderlines);
c) *Other littoral Baltic states*, as the Baltic area has become more of a region: *The Nordic welfare states*, which are committed to close co-operation and providing democratic and socially well-functioning models – while searching for a position in the 'new' Europe; and *Germany*, which has increased its regional position;
d) *International Institutions* focusing on the area. *The European Union* and *NATO* are the most crucial[4] and both are in the midst of enlargement.

Each of these relationships present both opportunities and challenges for the Baltics. The relationship with Russia, similar to other relationships between small states and adjacent regional powers e.g., Jordan and Iraq or Denmark and Germany, is bound to be 'a mixed bag'. Their relationship is further complicated by the fact that the Baltics were born out of the losing Soviet empire, and as such, are still in the process of ending former ties. Over the long-term, as this process draws to a close, complications should become evident. Unmistakably, the integration of the Baltic States into the world order – and most notably within the regional order – remains deeply intertwined with their relations to Russia.

Therefore, interactions with Russia appear to be the Baltics' greatest challenge. In the midst of the Russian reconstruction and adaptation to a new role as a major (regional) Eurasian power (rather than a global superpower), it is not clear for the Baltics what kind of Russia they need to relate to. On one hand, a 'revanchist' Russia could conceivably become a substantial threat to the Baltic States; whereas on the other hand, a co-operative Russia i.e., a Russia well-integrated into the world order, could prove an invaluable long-term partner in terms of increased prosperity and security in the area.

Russia maintains a series of specific interests regarding the Baltic States[5] : a) the achievement of friendly and peaceful relations on their Western border (major problems already exist on its Southern and Eastern borders); b) the access to the Baltic Sea as a littoral state (in light of Russia's few warm-water ports); c) the facilitation of the Kaliningrad issue (which threatens, physically, to suffocate Russian access to the West); and d) the societal conditions of Russian minorities within the Baltic States. It is extremely important to emphasise here that for Russia, its main concern is not to be isolated from the Baltic area.

Likewise, each of the Baltic states have unresolved and different problems with Russia: the border issue in Estonia; extensive Russian minorities in Estonia and Latvia; the Kaliningrad corridor in Lithuania; and sizeable commercial partnership ventures at stake in all three. In the short-term, none of them fear Russian intervention. However, their mutual relationship does play a major role in the Baltics' relations with the West. In the longer term, within the context of both uncertain developments inside Russia, and uncertainty as to whether the new world order destabilises or not, fears are that Russian intimidation and black-mail – and even aggression – could resurface. Conversely, in the event of controversies with the West, Russia still represents an alignment option.

Immediately after the Baltics' rebirth, all three states began cautiously pursuing 'unco-operative' policies toward Russia. As independence has consolidated, policies have presently shifted toward a more co-operative nature. Commercial dependencies have reappeared and Western demands for a series of Baltic conciliatory initiatives (concerning the minorities as an example) have been met. Though the development of a reasonable and co-operative relationship with Russia remains vaguely acceptable to many Balts, these relations may, in fact, assist their attempts at becoming even more attractive partners to European and American counterparts.

Preparation for membership of the European Union (EU) is currently another key challenge for the Baltic States. It is anticipated that membership would substantially improve their capabilities, while at the same time reduce their vulnerabilities vis-à-vis the EU states. The unipolar international arrangement currently favours efforts to overcome Cold War-related constraints regarding European and Eurasian co-operation. This is important in light of the growing demands placed on economic performance in the world markets. The international political transformation has been accompanied by economic shifts away from industrial ('Fordist') production to outputs based on high technology, service and flexibility (post-industrialism).

These market demands are especially difficult for the former memberstates of the Soviet Union. It urges the Baltics to either join the 'post-industrial club' or seize opportunities to fill specific economic roles in the larger community. Both choices could be assisted – and even accomplished – by successfully pursuing a co-operative integration into the EU. As Russia has its own problems with economic reform and adaptation, adherence to a Western economic model appears the one successful prototype to lean on. In the short term economic dependency on Russia also appears unattractive from a security standpoint.

The end of the Cold War left the EU with the vital challenge of expanding prosperity into the former Soviet sphere. This challenge was to be accomplished partly by enlargement and partly by encouraging their partners in the Soviet sphere to emulate social and economic infrastructures according to successful Western models. The danger of emulation, however, is that it may bring about societal instability (as was the traumatic case during the Iranian revolution following the Shah's attempts at modernisation along Western standards).

The Nordic political systems and welfare models, to date, have been adopted by the Baltics as sources of inspiration. Unlike the Baltics and their history of abrupt transformations and heterogeneous populations, Nordic countries are long characterised for their calm historical development and homogenous societies. Despite these differences, the Nordic models (together with the EU's concepts), may provide the Baltic States with further inspiration in building efficient social welfare infrastructures for the management of social problems and minority issues.

Since the time of their independence, the three Baltic states have actually been quite busy with respect to entering international agreements: they have successfully become member of a number of institutions (with many more applications pending). Integration for Estonia, Latvia and Lithuania has apparently taken place in a smooth, rapid and efficient manner. However, the issue of integration into the two most significant institutions of the Western community, NATO and the EU, still remains open, except for Estonia's inclusion in Agenda 2000: in the spring of 1997, Estonia was among the EU applicants selected for negotiation.

While the Baltics have openly and enthusiastically expressed their interests in becoming members of the EU and NATO, these organisations have not – in the early spring of 1997 – finalised any decision in favour of acceptance or rejection (neither have most of the EU and NATO memberstates). There is widespread belief in the West concerning the Baltic's imminent acceptance into the EU within some foreseeable timeframe, but not into NATO. What will be offered instead is a new and extended Partnership for Peace (PfP) programme (which is basically all of NATO minus the 'article five' guarantee). This new programme is labelled PfP 'Plus' (or 'Super').

When EU states appear rather favourable toward Baltic EU integration, their preference is often explained with a reference to two major points: a) that the Baltics represent new markets and may become part of a European division of labour; and b) that they can provide an 'entranceway' to Russian markets and its enormous economy. Reservations about integration concern 'how' and 'when', and are usually centred around the Baltics' internal need to transform themselves (economically and politically) in order to 'catch-up' to the EU system. As the relationship with Russia receives a much higher priority by major EU-countries, politically the EU has reservations regarding the Russian minorities. Similar to cases with former East European countries, the EU has taken advantage of opportunities to make demands on Baltic policy (cf. the Stability Pact). However, the Baltic States are small and their inclusion will thereby pose comparatively small political and economic problems for the EU.

A constructive relationship with Russia is, naturally, of supreme importance to the goals of NATO. Needing to balance their objective for broadening Western spheres of security with those of not wishing to provoke counterproductive political forces inside Russia, NATO members will maintain a particularly cautious stance as long as Russia remains in the throes of an internal transformation (where her prospects, politically, are inconclusive). The extended PfP programme may be interpreted as a reflection of this double balancing act because it neither excludes the Baltics from a Western security sphere[6], nor links their interests so closely as to intimidate Russia (a policy of chain-ganging perceived as intolerable).

Western efforts of adaptation, illustrated by the enlargement of its core institutions, NATO and the EU, are primarily concerned with broadening the sphere of security. The Western approach is based on a position of strength from being 'the winning side' and Russia 'the losing side' (though it includes a careful handling of a Russia whose nuclear arsenals remain intact). Although this relegates the small states of the Baltics to a subordinated role in Western policy, they, nonetheless, retain a strong incentive to join at available conditions. As a result of joining the winning side, they naturally would hope to rid themselves of Russian influence (and its potential blackmail) and, by reversing past capability deficits and specific incompatibilities related to their Soviet past, gain assistance in entering the new world order. The quest for adaptation thus provides the Baltics with a current motivation to become members of Western institutions.

These institutions may also provide the Baltic States with a framework for state-building and a direction for reconstruction. The initial phases of state-building are tense processes that often entail major internal problems. The approach to the EU will undoubtedly strengthen the victorious nationalist coalitions seeking to build 'Westernised' societies. Internationally, however, continuation along this path may provide the Baltics with a desired role in the new world order.

Neighbouring states have long been attentive and aware of these problems. In the future, however, the Baltics will need to continue to prove and promote their attractiveness as it should not be taken for granted that the perceived current attractiveness will last otherwise.

For all the Baltic Sea states, the period after the Cold War has been categorised by efforts of adjustment. It is has been a kind period, however, as none of the great regional powers have interfered with Baltic area policies. To the contrary, the greater powers have been satisfied with the smaller states (most prominently Denmark) to the point where they have allowed Denmark to fill 'the power vacuum' created by the retreat of the former Soviet Union (Hansen 1996). Along with the other Nordic countries, Denmark has been surprisingly attentive to the needs of the Baltic states. Although these relationships have developed in the absence of any significant regional power activity, it has occurred with the full understanding of the United States.

In more detailed studies, it becomes evident that Western views cannot be reduced to a single voice. However, the core Western institutions represent the 'condensation' of the members' view in terms of a least common denominator and thus reflect Western positions. Also within the Western community, cross-cutting views come to bear. One example is Carl Bildt's attempt to establish Russia's policy toward the Baltics as a 'litmus test' for the intentions of the new Russia (Bildt 1994).

Inside the Western community, the view of the United States is essential. As the most important actor in World politics, the US seeks to spread its own American World Order without the obstruction of equal adversaries. This Order, aimed at increasing American freedom of action, includes the maintainance and improvement of its international position as well as the spread of its economic (free-market) and political (democratic) models. According to the model for unipolarity, a unipole tends to encourage hard work from the small states as it is constantly subject to political exhaustion (as all management functions are likely left to the unipole). Furthermore, the other states are in a comparatively weak position to refuse the work: with no alternatives to leverage, they cannot turn to guarantees of security anywhere else. During periods of international unipolar stability, qualification for benefits is not linked to the containment of other poles, but rather, to the expansion of the unipole's winning model.

For the Baltic States, these considerations imply that their security guarantees are linked to their performance with respect to the expansion of the US World Order. To date, they receive a 'passing' profile for being in the process of adapting to the US (Western) models, attempting to join Western institutions and beginning to contribute to management functions i.e., the construction of the Baltic

Peacekeeping Batallion (of which an element has already been deployed in Bosnia as part of the Danish International Brigade).

As a consequence of their hard work and the disappearance of the zero-sum game, the Baltic Sea area is being subjected to an increased level of economic activity. Thus, in accordance with the quest for world market performance, they are expected to continue to focus work on this area as well as maintain a priority toward their relations with Russia, which, in the long run, could become more important than their current relations with the West. Finally, as the need and opportunity to join Western institutions has increased, though not yet to a full scale, the Baltics have certainly seized them.

External challenges

As previously argued, the most difficult challenge for the Baltic States (within the foreseeable future) is Russia. Their relationship may develop into one of co-operation and partnership, or one that may just as easily deteriorate. Beyond the efforts of the Baltics, successful management of the relationship depends upon Russia's own political development. The following are three possible scenarios for the structure of Russia's potential development:

a) The continuation of a peaceful and democratic development, which entails both its relationship with the West and further integration into the new world order;

b) The return of the 'White Czar', which signifies the aspirations of classic 'great power' ambitions;

c) The return of the 'Red Czar', which signifies renewed anti-Western fears together with an extroverted and expansionist strategy for the reconstruction of the empire.

These varying scenarios would naturally result in different security conditions for the Balts (as well as for the West), and thus provide them with differing alignment concerns.

If Russia continues its democratisation and integration in the world order, the Baltics' opportunity to break new ground with respect to Baltic-Russian co-operation will likely increase. Conversely, reservations derived from fear would be bound to decrease. Under this scenario, calls for a strong Western alignment would disappear. On the other hand, a close alignment with the West would hardly raise fears of Western entanglement in Russia, nor would it pose severe problems to the elite with respect to a 'revanchist', hard-line opposition.

Should the development of a White Czar or Red Czar re-emerge, this situation would clearly change. For the Balts, either would be considered a disastrous setback and lead, at the very least, to an increase in tensions. Perceptions of expansionist or aggressive intentions would increase the likelihood (Walt 1987) that Baltic efforts to align would become stronger.

For the West, however, there probably does exist a difference between a Red Czar and White Czar return. In the case of a Red Czar re-emergence, the West might opt to defend the Balts in order to avoid another 'classic' Cold War. A White Czar return, on the other hand, may cause lesser fear because Russia's great power ambitions are not necessarily a sufficient condition to cause the West to extend its defence lines. In such a case Russia might limit its ambitions to 'easier' and 'more approachable' objectives i.e., not daring to challenge the West directly. Consequently, the West would only have a minor incentive to extend its defence lines or increase the level of confrontation.

A fundamental question for the Baltic States to consider in all this realignment is: *When and how much can they trust the West?* A recent illustration of this question is striking: during the Kurdish uprising in Northeast Iraq in 1991, the Western signals of their intentions became blurred. It is probable that Kurdish leaders did not misperceive the direct US signals (though no promises as to the assistance for a Kurdish state were made), however the Kurdish people did not negotiate directly with US diplomats. Rather, the Kurds were encouraged and subsequently put pressure on their own leaders, causing the situation to spiral out of control.

There is obviously a large difference between the Kurdish scenario and the scenario for the Baltic States. Whereas the Kurds were given neither US support nor assurance in attempts to achieve a state, the Balts had full US support in reclaiming their independence, and they are subject to special attention from the unipole. In addition, being closer to the West in terms of stratification, the Balts have already been given far more Western attention than Eastern newcomers such as Kirgisystan.

In the first place US support is important, and in the case of unipolarity it is vital. In the second place, there is another dimension: Even though EU-membership is considered to be a soft one, the EU-states have strong reasons not to abandon a member state in trouble. They will be affected themselves, and they have formerly politically supported each other (as illustrated by the Falkland War).

As long as Western policy maintains its goal of expanding the Western security sphere, the Baltics are a part. However, if it comes to defend Western positions, the Baltics may fear they will not be included (cf. the scenarios above) or that they will end up as hostages or even a theatre. Such considerations may encourage the Baltics not to exclude Russia from their longer term alignment strategies.

Conversely for the West, a certain level of distrust of the Baltic States may exist. There are incentives for the Baltics to reconsider their relations with Russia (or choose differently), they possess a number of potential problems and are difficult to defend while bringing very little to the Western defence core. For the time being, any levels of distrust on the part of the Baltics are less important. As long as a unipolar environment exists, the likelihood of severe trials of strength internationally are low while the incentives to comply with the world order are high, also for Russia. "Force is least visible where power is is most fully and most adequately present. Power maintains an order; the use of force signals a possible breakdown" (Waltz 1979:185). In the longer term, however, distrust may regain its significance, most notably in the context of an emerging, structural change.

Security strategies available

Regarding security strategies, geopolitically small and weak states actually have three alternatives: *a) to opt for a close relationship with their major neighbour* (which they have become independent from); *b) to opt for neutrality* (the ability of self-defence is needed to boost credibility of such a choice); and *c) to align* (and thus add capabilities while reducing vulnerabilities).

As mentioned above alignment is the key option today: Presently, all three Baltic states are struggling to free themselves from their Soviet pasts in an effort to secure independence. Consequently, a 'too-intimate' relationship with Russia is ruled out. So is the option of neutrality as history has pointed to the deficits of such a strategy. Since none of the Baltic states are able to defend themselves (they do not even possess the potential), 'alignment' appears the proper choice[7]. In times when 'soft security' heads the international agenda, close economic and political co-operation – rather than actual military co-operation – appears the way forward. In time, this policy may shift. At present, however, the circumstances favour alignment; in fact, with the level of international tension where it is, conditions call for less dramatic terms of alignment. In addition, a series of important decisions were made immediately following each state's independence (certain decisions were taken even before independence was actually achieved). The decisions all pointed to a preference for alignment which included:

- Multilevel and issue co-operative political and economic initiatives;
- Applications for membership of core Western institutions; and
- Security activities (including military agreements) in close co-operation with other states.

Because of a relative lack of capabilities and the fact that Western policy compensates toward Russia, the outcome of these strategic decisions (all dependent on a Western approach) forced the Baltics to be reactive. This is reflected in the apparent limits of an alignment strategy for the Baltics i.e., the West has been reluctant to be drawn into any type of chain-gang with the Baltic States. NATO, in particular, has remained reluctant to risk becoming part of any conflict arising from Baltic-Russian troubles. As the foremost instrument of the winning Western coalition, NATO is in pursuit of a Western sphere of security. For the moment, however, Baltic membership of NATO does not seem achievable. In its place, an extended Partnership for Peace programme will probably be offered by NATO to encourage the link between the Baltics and the West while at the same time avoiding a chain-gang or provoking of Russia. For the time being, though, the sharp line between NATO and not-NATO is being challenged, and the ongoing transformation of NATO into a security organization rather than a classic defense alliance (Heurlin 1990) may down-grade the problem. One indication of the softening of the line is the U.S. Baltic Action Plan, which aims at integrating the Balts in the US World Order by preparing them for EU membership, and the extension of the PfP-programme. Some of the new PfP activities are being 'NATO-fied', and cooperation between NATO and the partners is intensified.

Although the prospect of not becoming full members in the first round of NATO enlargement may cause frustration and disappoint-ment within the Baltic States, the limit seems compatible with the dynamics of the current world order and, therefore, explicable by the analytical framework. In times of comparatively low international tension, states expectedly refrain from offering security guarantees (if such guarantees are perceived to be connected with any risk or use). On the other hand, periods of 'soft security' and unipolarity favour increased international and regional co-operation respectively. These dynamics point out why the Baltic States are being integrated, politically and economically, as well as why the military alignment faces certain limits. If Russia should suddenly shift its strategy for reconstruction to an expansionist one (thus challenging the world order), the West would naturally have to reconsider the Baltics' status – in either direction. On the other hand, should Russia become a well-integrated member of the world order, NATO would likely open up to the Baltics (as memberships become less risky and useful). A strategy for co-operative security thus seems the most obvious choice for each of the Baltic states, at least in terms of the present international dynamics where soft rather than hard co-operation, and low levels of tension, exist.

Before a conclusion on the strategic prospects for the Baltics can be reached, one further question, regarding the dimension of 'balancing', should be addressed: *Has the end of the Cold War put an end to balancing in international politics?* In the Baltics' case, the current world order and lower levels of tension have obviously downgraded the relative significance of this dimension. However, balancing incentives remain in other areas: *firstly,* within the mutual relations of the Baltics; *secondly,* within relations between the Baltics on one side, and the West vis-à-vis Russia on the other; and *thirdly,* between the Baltic States and the individual European states. It has often been noted that the Baltic States are more likely to co-operate externally than mutually. Moreover, in cases of mutual co-operation, they tend to be brought together by third parties e.g., the Danish initiative concerning the Baltic Peacekeeping Batallion, as well as the Baltic Sea initiatives.

Rather than working alone, it appears the Baltic States have two incentives for accepting external (Western) demands for mutual co-operation: firstly (and the urgent priority), their commitment to becoming part of the Western community; and secondly, their acceptance can be considered part and parcel of their bargain with the West (which does not desire any inter-Baltic troubles). Consequently, in an effort to please the West, the Baltics, must demonstrate mutually co-operative activity.

In spite of this aim, major obstacles prevent each from whole-heartedly engaging in such mutual co-operation. From an outsider's viewpoint, the Baltics' specific and individual societal strategies could possibly become endangered by being regarded as one unit. It is worth noting once again that, indeed, these three states are different and hence, maintain differing positions vis-à-vis the Western community.

Lithuania holds the better record with respect to political standards while their Russian minority is smaller than both Latvia's and Estonia's. From a Lithuanian point of view, NATO differentiation regarding membership of the Baltic States would be preferable. On the other hand, the Russian corridor running through Lithuania holds the key to potential Russian-Lithuanian troubles. Conversely, owing to the economic performance of Estonia, EU differentation was preferable, and Estonia's inclusion in Agenda 2000 was evidence of that.

At this point, a question must be raised concerning the strategic choices: Should the Baltic States subordinate their individual needs in order to pursue a policy of improved mutual relations or should they focus on their own needs and problems? It is often argued that in order for the Baltics to improve their mutual relations, as well as their relations with third parties, there must exist a deeper level of co-operation between Estonia, Latvia and Lithuania[8]. However, the Baltics remain most attracted by co-operation with Western countries than with each other. Their mutual relationships thus seems to forward some kind of balancing positions.

To claim that states which contribute to the US World Order are better off than those which do not is an understatement; partnership with the United States is clearly a decisive asset. Obtaining a general security guarantee from the US requires a compliance with the US World Order which includes: a) a strong US request for stable regional set-ups; b) free access to all waters (including the Baltic Sea); c) an expansion of the model of democracy and free market; and d) a reasonable partnership with Russia (still a strong and nuclearised regional power). The US pursues its policy in the Baltic Sea region accordingly, and the Baltics so far have complied with the world order.

Present conditions favour the organisation of long-term regional stability and security. Just 'how much' and 'how far' co-operation should extend is the subject of current political debate. In the West's perception, Baltic progress should lean toward integrative efforts, responsible co-operation and open-minded adjustment. For the time being, security conditions for the three Baltic States analytically seem to favour the strategy of *co-operative security* (Heurlin 1995 and 1997). If this assumption is correct, the means should be subject to further attention. In order to pursue both internal as well as external objectives, the circumstantial account so far favours means to ensure that:

- further transformation of Baltic societies in terms of market and democracy takes place smoothly and rapidly (with as much support from all groups of citizens as possible);
- aggregate Baltic capabilities are raised to improve external attractiveness while vulnerabilities i.e., internal tensions, are diminished in order to avoid threats of becoming future political or military battlefields.
- securing peaceful relations with all neighbourstates which will reduce losses of autonomy as well as providing the broadest basis possibly to achieve optimal benefits from resources in a context of introvert development.

In assessing the proper strategic framework by which to achieve these objectives, a balanced co-operative security appears to be the one. Although a co-operative security is well suited, this paragraph adds the term 'balanced' co-operative security to include the notion of preparing for potential longer term conflicts, as well as for increasing marginal returns on the current base of resources. Specifically, the notion refers to an increased priority concerning relations with Russia. Networks of co-operation across East and West are of tremendous significance in order to offset Russian isolation; the Baltic States are centrally situated in such a network.

Historically the Baltic States, situated between East and West, have always been urged to choose – or forced to choose – between the two sides. After 1989, however, the Baltics, rather than settling for being a 'piece of the puzzle', may turn their role into a 'bridge'. By taking a co-operative approach, the Baltics can conceivably obtain a key position in the Baltic region by becoming 'the bridge' between the core of Europe and Russia. As the Baltics' major security concern lies with its relations to Russia, such an approach is likely to prove beneficial. With the past holding such a prominent consideration for many citizens in the Baltic states, it is evident that the position 'as a bridge' is difficult one. However, it is important to stress that all the components of the Baltic security equation have changed from the time of the Cold War; the same can be said for all the components of their future welfare and prosperity. A 'one bridge' strategy is thus a double-edged sword for the Baltics, reflecting the pros and cons of their appearance as one unit, or as three distinct units. Consequently, it points to the significance of a balancing dimension (though not the most important dimension) in a proper security strategy.

Summary: a balanced co-operative security

It has been argued that post-1989 changes have been favourable to the Baltic States. In an attempt to establish and adapt themselves to the interstate community, the changes have provided them with a unique international goodwill. In addition, their primary security concerns (for the foreseeable future) compromise their relationship with Russia. The present lack of threats increases the Baltics' internal ability to care for their positions, hence reducing their vulnerabilities.

The Baltic States' difficulty in re-emerging on the international scene, and their respective pain factor in undergoing necessary internal transformations, cannot not be downplayed. However, in the process of transformation and international establishment, the easing of differences between their needs and the demands of reshaped Western policies, provide a unique (and perhaps one-time) window of opportunity.

Naturally, there are obvious problems connected to the situation of Estonia, Latvia and Lithuania. Being geographically adjacent to an empire in the process of decline is a matter of serious security concern. Furthermore, emerging from a losing system, their internal arrangements are vulnerable. As has been emphasized, their demographic composition makes them potentially unstable. On balance, however, Baltic efforts seem to be leading toward becoming part of the post-1989 interstate community at levels exceeding their innate positions of weakness.

The condition of unipolarity, together with the process of regionalisation and the present soft international agenda allows room for the harder working weaker states to contribute and benefit. Specifically, the US' unique global position and the EU's regional position require the Baltics to develop a reasonable relationship with Russia and fulfil the role as 'Eurasian bridge'. Therefore, a soft, civil and multilateral integration i.e., a strategy for co-operative security, thus appears the Baltics' best approach for the foreseeable future. It is important, moreover, that each of the Baltic states incorporates a 'balancing' dimension of co-operative security in order to secure their individual needs as well as a whole range of strategic options over the long run. Complying with these and other guidelines i.e., actively joining the world order, should position them to make the most of Western (sphere of security) enlargement efforts.

In the context of a unipolar theoretical analysis, a sequence of conclusions can be summarised as follows:

1 Unipolarity offers the Baltic States a favourable security environment.

2 Due to capability deficiencies, the Baltics are inclined to seek co-operation.

3 'Soft' alignment is one characteristic of co-operation.

4 The Baltics are prone to 'soft' alignment.

5 A sphere of 'harder' security may reoccur.

6 In the event of 'harder times' i.e., international tensions, the Baltics will need a 'hard' alignment.

7 As small states adjacent to a major power, the Baltics, in a period of international tension, are predisposed to considering a close relationship with Russia.

8 Accordingly, a level of mistrust may occur between the West and the Baltic States (especially in the event of a 'Red Czar' return).

9 Hence, the current international climate favours co-operation between the West and the Baltics according to a 'balanced co-operative security'.

These conclusions hopefully serve to add perspective to the current debates which focus on available courses of action for the Baltic States with respect to available security strategy alternatives. Though the long-term prospects for enhancement appear bleak, they are not necessarily so: they must be taken in the context of the whole.

Notes

1 The model assumes no 'rational behaviour' (cf. Waltz 1979), neither does it preclude processes without any friction. It just points at essential conditions which tend to be met by the states and deeply challenge states which do not adapt.

2 The concept of the West (the United States and EU) is adopted in this analysis. However, it could be questioned as could other international identities after 1989.

3 For a discussion of post-industrialism, see Drucker 1993.

4 It should be noted that international institutions are dealt with as actors as they are viewed as state co-operation within a soft alignment. They are, however, analysed as 'dependent' actors i.e., their functioning depends on the strategies of the memberstates.

5 For a full treatment of Russia's policy toward the Baltic region, see Jönsson 1994 and 1997.

6 'Security sphere' conceptualizes the spread of the unipole's ambitions and order as opposed to interests that attempt to demarcate these ambitions and order toward an adversary.

7 Neutrality under a unipolar structure is of course assigned a different context than under a bipolar structure. If a state belongs to the

unipolarised realm (a matter of belonging to the level of processes), unipolar neutrality comes down to the question of choosing to adhere to the world order or not. The only additional choice is actual challenge.
8 Here again, the methods of Nordic countries may serve as a model. There is a common Nordic understanding that the most useful way of relating, rather than creating an actual community, is by a commitment *not to complicate* the security policy of another (Bajarūnas 1995:9).

References

Bajarūnas, Eitvydas: 'Lithuania's security dilemma'. *Chaillot Papers* 19, 1995.

Bildt, Carl: 'The Baltic Litmus Test'. *Foreign Affairs*, Vol. 73:5, 1994.

Christensen, Thomas J., and Jack Snyder: 'Chain gangs and passed bucks: Predicting alliance patterns in multipolarity'. *International Organization*, Vol. 44:2, 1990.

Drucker, Peter F.: *Managing for the Future*. Butterworth Heinemann Ltd., Oxford 1993.

Ham, Peter Van: 'The Baltic States: Security and Defense after Independence'. *Chaillot Papers* 19, 1995.

Hansen, Birthe: *Unipolarity – a Theoretical Model*. Working Paper 10. Institute of Political Science, University of Copenhagen, Copenhagen 1993.

Hansen, Birthe: *Unipolarity and the Middle East*. University of Copenhagen, Copenhagen 1995.

Hansen, Birthe: Dansk Baltikumpolitik 1989–1995. *Dansk Udenrigspolitisk Årbog 1995*, DUPI, København 1996.

Heurlin, Bertel: *NATO, Europa, Danmark: Perspektiver for 90'erne*. SNU, Copenhagen 1990.

Heurlin, Bertel: 'NATO, Security, and the Baltic States: A New World, A new Security, a New NATO. In *Hansen and Heurlin 1997*.

Heurlin, Bertel: 'The Baltic Region and the New Security Dynamics'. In *Joenniemi and Stålvant 1995*.

Joenniemi, Pertti, and Carl-Einar Stålvant (eds.): *Baltic Sea Politics. Achievements and Challenges*. Nordic Council, Stockholm 1995.

Jonson, Lena: 'Russia and the Near Abroad'. In *Hansen and Heurlin 1997*.

Jonson, Lena: *Rysk Politik i Nordeuropa – det baltiska dilemmat*. Världpolitikens Dagsfrågor 4, UI, Stockholm 1994.

Morrow, James D.: 'Alliances and Asymmetry: An Alternative to the Capability Aggregation Model'. *American Journal of Political Science*, Vol. 35:4, 1991.

Snyder, Glenn H.: 'The Security Dilemma in Alliance Politics'. *World Politics*, Vol. XXXVI:4, 1984.

Walt, Stephen M.: *The Origins of Alliances*. Cornell University Press, Ithaca 1987.

Waltz, Kenneth N.: *Theory of international politics*. Random House, New York 1979.

Chapter 6

Russia and the "near abroad"

Concepts and Trends

Lena Jonson

The Baltic States and the "Gap" in Russian Politics

The purpose of this chapter is to critically analyse Russia's policy toward its "near abroad", and the position of the Baltic states in relation to this policy. It will be argued that a gap exists between, on the one hand, Russian ambitions on the former Soviet territory, and on the other hand, the hard facts of the post-Soviet realities which do not always allow these ambitions to be implemented. So far, this gap has had a moderating influence on Russian policy. However, the gap also makes Russian policy unpredictable in regard to the means with which this gap is to be bridged: by adapting to reality or by forcing reality to adapt. The Baltic states are not members of the CIS, and according to official Russian statements, not part of the near abroad either. A question to discuss here is to what extent Russian policy towards the CIS also reveals its ambitions towards the Baltic states.

Within this context, Russia's policy toward the independent Baltic states will be discussed. The future of the Baltic states is to a large extent dependent on how Russian policy tries to bridge the gap.

Integration within the CIS will be chosen as a case in the analysis of Russian policy toward the near abroad. In the first section, basic concepts in Russian foreign policy since the formation of a consensus in 1993 will be discussed. This is followed by an analysis of the results from Russian policy on integration, and a discussion of bridging the gap. In a final part, tentative conclusions are drawn from this analysis with regard to Russian policy toward the Baltic states.

A basic consensus in the making

Concepts

At the core of the foreign policy consensus which replaced heated controversies between the President and Parliament in 1992[1] was the process of formulating the national and strategic interests of the new Russian state. Russian policy immediately after the break-up of the Soviet Union can be characterised as "withdrawal" in the sense that the government wanted to cut down all costly economic and military engagement outside its new state borders.[2] Domestic economic reforms had highest priority; economic aspects predominated, and eventual military, strategic and geo-political interests had only low priority. Russia, who had taken responsibility over those former Soviet troops that were not nationalised by the new states, declared its troops to be withdrawn. Consequently, troops were pulled back from the hot spot of Nagorno-Karabakh as well as from Azerbaijan. At this time, a withdrawal from the Baltic states was also initiated.

During the first year after the break-up of the Soviet Union, Russia was passive in relation to the new independent states. Instead of actively promoting an integrationist policy on new conditions within the CIS, Russia itself became occupied with its statebuilding process. There was also confusion over what Russia 'is' and where Russia was heading. The Yeltsin government was soon heavily criticised by the Opposition. Well before the December 1993 Parliamentary elections, a shift in policy statements started to become evident. A consensus regarding the fundamentals of foreign policy was developing within the Russian political elite. The outcome of the elections made the shift more urgent.

The shift can to a large extent be explained by the power struggle on the domestic scene. However, at the roots of this consensus was also a new awareness of the problems following from the break-up of the former common infrastructure, and of the new vulnerabilities and threats to Russian security. Already the draft of the Russian military doctrine published in May 1992 spotted the main threat as coming from regional armed conflicts close to Russia's new borders. Such conflicts developed in Tajikistan, Georgia/South Ossetia and Abkhazia, Moldova/Transdniestr, and Azerbaijan/Nagorno-Karabakh. There was also a fear that Russia's new weakened position would be further undermined by the new states orienting themselves away from Russia and that states from outside the former Soviet territory would strengthen their influence. And here a crucial point can be made: In its search for identity and an international role, Russia returned after a short time of confusion and soon claimed itself as a great power.

A central element of the new consensus became the very idea that Russia was still a great power and had to be respected as such. In 1993 the "near abroad" was defined as a "historic sphere of interest" and Russia's role within this region was considered a precondition for Russian great power status. However, times had changed and the content of the new great power role had to be defined in a different way than before. The former superpower had to adapt to a more modest role – and exactly what that would include was difficult to define.

During 1993, Russian policy became more active in preventing the disintegration of the former Soviet territory by interfering on the domestic scenes of conflict-ridden states to Russia's south. Such ways included: efforts to integrate the new states both in the CIS and via a web of bilateral agreements; preparedness to take on responsibility for peacekeeping and conflict resolution in the former Soviet territory; and reorganising Russian military presence in the new states into treaty-based military bases.[3] In order to get the new states back on track, Russia played on their weaknesses. Georgia, which attempted to stay out of the CIS and avoid Russian dominance, provides an example. By meddling in the Georgia-Abkhazia conflict, Russia increased the vulnerability of the Georgian regime in 1993. In exchange for Russia's support against the Abkhazi offensive in August and September 1993, Georgia became a member of the CIS, signed the Tashkent Treaty on Collective Security as well as a treaty on friendship and co-operation which included an agreement for Russian military bases to be allowed on Georgian territory.[4] A similar pattern can be found when Azerbaijan, weakened by the domestic turmoil following the conflict around Nagorno-Karabakh, returned to the CIS and also signed the Tashkent Treaty on Collective Security in 1993.[5]

With regard to the near abroad, two main objectives were established: 1) to attain control over the former Soviet territory; and 2) to deny "outsiders" (states outside the former Soviet Union) a strategic position on this territory. These objectives were already reflected in April 1993 in the guidelines on foreign policy issued by the Russian Security Council, as well as in statements by President Yeltsin and Foreign Minister Andrei Kozyrev.[6] Nonetheless, scepticism against formulating any foreign policy doctrine on the part of Kozyrev, and rejection by Duma of any foreign policy draft from the

Foreign Ministry in 1992 and 1993, reflected the complicated process of attaining a consensus.

Already by the May 1992 draft of the Russian military doctrine (signed in its final version in November 1993), the question of the "near abroad" as a zone of special interest to Russia was raised by the declaration that the defence of Russian minorities in these countries was a task for the Russian military.[7]

Not until September 1995 was a proper policy document on the "near abroad" issued.[8]. In President Yeltsin's decree "Russian Strategy with regard to the Member States of the CIS", the near abroad was given first priority to Russia's national security and strategic interests.[9] The document declared as Russia's main purposes the strengthening of Russia as a leading force on former Soviet territory, and the integration of this territory. It envisaged integration in the economic, security and humanitarian fields.

The document clearly declared the CIS as a zone of Russian interest to which outsiders were not allowed. Consequently, the CIS would act as a joint bloc against the outside world. "When co-operating with third countries and international organisations, Russia should make them realise that this region is, above all, a Russian zone of interest". It stressed that CIS states "must be persuaded to stand by the obligation not to participate in any alliances and blocs directed against any of these states". The CIS was also to act as a united bloc in relation to the outside world, to "work out common positions on international issues and co-ordinate their actions on the international arena" and agree on their positions in the UN and in relations with NATO, the EU and the Council of Europe.

The decree reflected a certain aggressiveness in its determination to attain its objectives, but also a larger flexibility on how to attain them. It described an integration model where the member states themselves chose the tempo of integration and degree of closeness to the organisation. However, it also stressed that "the attitude of our partners to this model will be a major factor in determining the extent of economic, political and military support from Russia". With regard to the Russian minorities in the CIS, it stated, "In the events of human rights violations in the CIS countries, Russia may – as a penalty – make financial, economic, military, political and other co-operation with each particular state conditional upon its treatment of the Russians on its territory".

The need for closing ranks under Russian leadership had been pointed out in September 1994 in a report by the Russian Federal

Intelligence Service (SVR) under its director Yevgenii Primakov. The report, "Russia-CIS: Does the Western Position Need Correction?", pointed to the threat of foreign influence on CIS territory and argued in favour of economic, political and military integration.[10] The report discussed three future scenarios, two of which included threats from foreign influences. In the first case, separatist forces would achieve an upper hand with direct or indirect assistance from abroad, initiating destabilisation which might lead to the break-up of states. In the second case, a split-up of the CIS following from subregional integration (without Russia) would lead to groups of states shutting themselves off, further prodding them towards "external centres of influence". The report perceived the situation as Russia's position being threatened by the influence from the outside not only on its Western flank, but even more so on its southern borders, in the Caucasus and Central Asia.

In January 1996, the controversial Foreign Minister Kozyrev resigned and was succeeded by Yevgenii Primakov. Primakov was respected in different political camps for being a determined and consequent follower of Russian interest, but still not a hawk. With great knowledge in foreign affairs from his academic career as an expert on the Middle East and Islam, he seemed better fitted for handling relations with countries in the "near" and "far abroad" than his predecessor. In his first interview as the new foreign minister in January 1996, he stressed the CIS' importance to Russia and as the highest priority, presented the need to strengthen integrationist tendencies on the former Soviet territory and to stabilise the region with regard to armed conflicts.[11] With Primakov as foreign minister, Russia thus seemed to have reached a firm and determined consensus on basic concepts of Russian policy toward its "near abroad".

Strategic Interests and National Security: Back to an Old Framework?

Gorbachev had introduced a new approach to strategic interests and national security, and Yeltsin developed this approach in his policy toward the West. That policy was build on international co-operation along common interests as well as security needs and integration in international organisations.[12]

The shift in the Russian understanding of co-operation and common interests with the West – from the euphoria of 1991–92 into a more critical stance in 1993 – can to a certain extent be considered a step in the direction of realism. Russian national and strategic interests were considered specific, different and only partly overlapping with Western or American interests; thus Russia declared it would pursue its own interests.

However, there was also a shift in the way the international situation was perceived. Becoming increasingly concerned with its international status as a great power, Russia became more concerned with the competitive element within international co-operation. With strong roots in Soviet tradition, a hard core "realism" existed as an alternative approach to international politics. Here the world was perceived as a zero-sum game where, by definition, what was won by one side was lost by the other; and where the West – and especially the US – were looked upon with a suspicion that had to be countered by the formation of balancing coalitions. With the new consensus developing, Russia seemed to be partly sliding back into a more traditional way of looking at security.[13]

With a debate on strategic interests and national security running high, it was not until April 1996 that a draft of a Russian national security policy was published.[14] It had been under preparation for one and a half year, and several institutes and departments had been involved in the preparations.[15] The document was later presented in a slightly revised version in a speech by President Yeltsin in June 1996.[16]

In February 1996 Yurii Baturin, Yeltsin's adviser for national security and responsible for the draft, announced that a general doctrine on national security was being worked out on the basis of which a strategy for the "coming 50, 70 or even 100 years" would be formulated, as well as a policy for the nearest five years. Not all of this material was to be made public. These documents are interesting for their perception of the world and trends in international politics. It would of course be a serious exaggeration to say that these policy documents on Russian national security reflected a traditional Soviet zero-sum understanding of the world. However, there was a tendency in that direction.

Yeltsin stressed a competitive element in US-Russian relations, "The international system searches for a new pivotal point simultaneously in three dimensions: the geopolitical, the geo-strategic and the geo-economic". According to him, the world had not become more simple, more secure or without conflicts. The complete draft dealt with international rivalry and geo-political strife. "There is a clear trend on the part of the Muslim world and the West to oppose integration within the CIS because they are not interested in the

117

re-emergence of a serious political and economic rival in whatever form". The draft more clearly pointed to an emerging geo-political situation where Russia, step by step, was losing its influence in the region of the former Soviet territory. It further stated that to Russia's east "a fierce struggle for dominance and influence takes place in Central Asia between China, Turkey, Iran, Pakistan (and even Afghanistan), Saudi Arabia, USA and NATO countries". The US was accused of supporting Turkey's bid to play a more important role in the region. An arch of instability spanned over Central Asia and the Caucasus with the possible consequence of a formation of a "buffer zone of states in the Southeast which are anything but friendly toward Russia". To Russia's west, in Europe, a new geo-political situation was being created by former Soviet allies being drawn into the West's military-political sphere, thereby creating "a new geo-political situation in Europe".

The draft introduced to the centres of the world the policy of "equal distance". Primakov explained this in an interview in December 1996: "The US is still the leading power in a military and economic sense, but will soon be passed economically by the European Union. During the next century China, Japan and Southeast Asia will add to the list of strong centres. During these conditions we have to follow a diversified policy which is oriented toward co-operation with all, and simultaneously, we must not ally ourselves with any specific pole".[17] In the press, a more outspoken analysis of a geo-political and zero-sum world view could be found.[18]

In spite of simultaneously being considered a pragmatic politician and in favour of international co-operation, Primakov's world view is to a large extent coloured by a perspective of rivalry and competition between the great powers. Within this perspective an eventual NATO enlargement is perceived in Moscow.

Integration in the CIS

Russian Policy

The issue of CIS integration illustrates a gap in Russian politics. Integration is crucial for Russia's future status and has been designated as a priority issue for Russian policy. However, the Russian leadership has no specific idea of how integration should be furthered.

In efforts to formulate such a policy, three crucial questions had to be faced: How to promote integration?; How to uphold a Russian leading role?; and What price is Russia prepared to pay for its geo-strategic interests on former Soviet territory?

The Russian leadership had problems finding the balance between the need for integration and the rational choice of avoiding all obligations that may be harmful to Russia's own economic development. Yeltsin's words in his speech to Parliament in February 1994 reflected this dilemma when stating that "Integration must not bring harm to Russia itself or lead to an overstretch of our forces and resources, material as well as financial".[19]

The Russian "isolationists" from the early 1990s had made it a crucial argument that Russia ought not take on obligations that are costly. Thus, they recommended withdrawal from all costly military-political involvement and economic subsidising. With the ambition of strengthening the position as the great power in the region, the geo-strategic concerns became more important to the Russian leaders, and they became somewhat more prepared to pay the economic costs. How to build up and maintain a leading position became a central question.

In an unofficial document from 1994, "Strategy for Russia", an independent group of researchers, politicians, business people and military officers led by Sergei Karaganov argued that "Russia should not carry out its leading role by administrative control".[20] Their vision came close to the role of a hegemon upholding a dominant influence in a region but without taking on costly obligations. The authors coined the slogan "leadership instead of administrative control, economic dominance instead of political responsibility".

In April 1996, a new document by the group was published "Will the union be restored?: Prospects for post-Soviet space."[21] The new document stated that Russia's own economic development and internal stability must decide the tempo of CIS integration, and that Russia ought not to take on expenses thereby hoping to speed up the integration. The authors suggested a functional approach to integration where co-operation develops from below rather than from the top and with regard to specific issues and sectors. They warned of Russia taking upon military-political obligations and thereby being forced to spend military and economic resources in order to save an ally. According to their views, since the countries concerned have no alternatives, integration would take place sooner or later. Some CIS states would prefer being closer to Russia, while others would not. The authors therefore suggested a differentiated policy to the CIS-countries.

The document was thus in sharp contrast with spring 1996 loud declarations by the Russian government concerning new stages of deeper economic co-operation with Belorussia, Kazakhstan, and Kyrgyzstan. The new integration structures, hastily proclaimed, gave a hint of a desperate search for results in CIS integration.

An Integrated CIS?

Today, all former Soviet republics (except the Baltic states) are members of the CIS;[22] nine are members of the Tashkent Treaty on Collective Security, and nine have Russian troops on their territory.[23]

Russia thus managed to secure its position on the former Soviet territory in the sense that it stopped the process of rapid reorientation by the newly independent states. However, to continue integrating these states turned out to be a thorny and complicated process in which Russia was less successful.

Russia had to take into consideration the scepticism against CIS integration by the other member states, and to adapt its policy accordingly. As an international organisation, the CIS was envisioned by Russian leadership as a future supra-state character rather than an inter-state character.[24] However, reality forced Moscow into a policy of only inter-state agreements because nothing else was accepted by the CIS. Difficulties in developing multilateral co-operation with the CIS has also made bilateral agreements between Russia and the individual states much more significant.

Resistance within the organisation allows for only a slow and gradual integration whereby individual states are free to choose the degree of closeness to the organisation and the tempo of the process. The decision-making structure is loose and states are permitted to abstain from participating in decisions. While decisions are taken by unanimity, a state can abstain from voting and will thus not be tied to the decision. States can also make reservations to the text of the decision when their national parliaments ratify the document. This procedure undermines the authority of most CIS documents. Even when signed, most decisions are not implemented.

Military Integration: The embryo of a defence organisation was created by the Tashkent Treaty of Collective Security on 15 May 1992. However, only six states at that time signed the treaty (Russia, Armenia, Kazakstan, Kyrgyzstan, Tajikistan and Uzbekistan) and in late 1993, Azerbaijan, Georgia and Belorussia joined. Most states did not ratify the treaty until 1995.

Articles 1 and 2 of the treaty commit the signatories to refrain from the use of force in their relations and establishes the need to consult each other on all important security matters. Article 3 establishes a collective security council consisting of the heads of participating states and the commander of the CIS joint armed forces. Article 4 establishes the principle of mutual assistance in the case of aggression. The remaining Articles 5 through 11 address the question of military co-ordination to repulse aggression, stress implementing the treaty's provisions in accordance with the principles of the UN Charter, and provide for a treaty life of five years.[25]

Military integration did not follow. The status of the treaty was unclear. Constructed as a defence alliance against external threats, it was thus of less help in local wars between or within member states. At the time of the creation of the CIS in December 1991, Russia had tried to keep the common military forces intact. The CIS Joint Military Command, established in the end of December 1991, was dissolved in summer 1993 and replaced by a CIS Joint Military Coordinating Council. As national armies were organised in all former Soviet republics, the interest for military integration waned. Bilateral military agreements therefore play a central role.

In his September 1995 decree on "Russian strategy with regard to members of the CIS", Yeltsin declared that a system of collective security was to be created based on both the Tashkent Treaty of Collective Security (from 15 May 1992), and the bilateral agreements between Russia and individual CIS members.[26] He stated that the Tashkent Treaty would develop into a defence union, military infrastructure facilities would be preserved, the external borders of the CIS strengthened, the presence of Russian border troops in these countries guaranteed by mutual agreements, joint efforts in peace-keeping operations secured, and, also, that the CIS states were obliged "not to participate in any alliances and blocs directed against any of these states".

The resistance within the CIS to developing military co-operation is strong. Most states do not want to establish any permanent military structures or forces. All co-operation therefore has the character of temporary measures such as decisions on "peacekeeping" operations in Tajikistan, and Abkhazia on a six-months mandate basis. Most states do not want to send troops or contribute financially.

With regard to the discussions on NATO enlargement, even if Russian voices had repeatedly warned that the Tashkent Treaty as an answer will be turned into a proper military alliance, there is still a long way until such an organisation can be created.

Russia has so far been successful in its efforts to promote CIS military co-operation only with regard to the defence of CIS outer borders[27], a common air-defence system[28], military-industrial co-operation, and peacekeeping. In order to promote a common approach Russia has introduced conceptual documents on conflict regulation,[29] collective security,[30] and agreements on CIS peace-keeping.[31]

Russia secured its military relations mainly by bilateral agreements. These included agreements on military co-operation, co-operation on border controls, on military bases legitimising Russian military presence on the soil of these states,[32] or Russian contributions to the build-up of the defence. In so doing, Russia again paid less attention to economic considerations and the enormous drain on Russian resources.

Economic integration: In his speech of March 1993, Yeltsin presented a plan for economic integration in which he proposed: the gradual process of a free trade zone; the creation of a proper economic union; a customs union; and a payment and currency union. In September 1993 a CIS declaration of intent was taken on the step-by-step creation of an Economic Union. Nothing materialised however.

In his September 1995 decree on Russian strategy in relation to the CIS member states, Yeltsin listed as priority areas for co-operation with CIS countries: the broadening of the customs union, the creation of a payments union and the establishment of a single capital market. The decree also recommended that the broadening of the customs union by admitting countries linked to Russia "with deeply integrated economic relations and strategic political partnership", was one of the most important ways of strengthening the CIS.[33]

However, not until 1995 did Belorussia and Kazakhstan join Russia in a CIS Customs Union; in February 1996 Kyrgyzstan followed. Moreover, due to the degree of difficulty in creating a customs union, when a new agreement on further economic co-operation was signed between the four states on 29 March 1996, they were still in an early phase of setting up a customs union arrangement.[34] The March 1996 agreement stated the intention to create a common market for goods, services, capital and labour, a common system on property and use of property, price policy, the civil code and state regulations of the economy.

The Russian independent press pointed out the declaratory nature of the integration between the four states, questioning the economic advantages. The trade between these countries had sharply fallen since the dissolution of the Soviet Union. For Russia, trade with the CIS countries constituted only 21% of foreign trade in 1995 and did not dominate the foreign trade of these countries. It was pointed out in the press that since the precondition of Russian dominance would not be accepted, these countries were unable to create a unitary rouble zone with a common policy under a central bank. What these four states had agreed on could not be attractive to the other CIS states.[35] Instead, there were other factors of a political and geopolitical nature behind the agreement.[36]

Two weeks after the four-state agreement was signed, Yeltsin's words that "the pace of the expanding, new organisation should not be forced" and that the four states should "stand on their own legs first" before inviting others to join them, was a clear indication of the troubles of implementation.[37] Political and geopolitical factors may explain the agreement.[38] Belorussia, Kazakhstan and Kirgizia were in desperate need of favourable Russian credits, and Russia wanted good conditions for its military presence in these countries. Even the Russian-Belorussian treaty, which was signed with much ado on 2 April 1996, was considered as nothing but a declaration of intent.

Bridging the gap? Russian policy means

In spite of the importance in Russian policy statements given to CIS integration, the outcome so far has been bleak.[39] Thus, between Russian ambitions of integrating the CIS under Russian leadership, and the post-Soviet reality, there is a gap which does not allow for this.

There is a stable but slow trend toward co-operation in which several factors contribute: first of all, the former Soviet republics are dependent on Russia through the common Soviet heritage; secondly, Russia has been pushing in favour of co-operation; thirdly, Russia has the strongest economy in the region. When the Russian economy does recover, Russia may well become a motor in the economic development of the region, and thus CIS integration may appear more attractive to its members.

However, today several factors prevent a rapid integration. First, Russia's weakness – in a political, economic and military sense. Its political weakness is reflected in the lack of a policy able to fulfil the declared objectives in relation to the "near abroad" in general, and to integration specifically. So far, Russian policy can be characterised as having a rather 'ad hoc' nature which mainly reacts to current events. The Russian economy is too weak to be able to use economic measures as foreign policy expedients. Russia can not expand its influence by investing in the near abroad or strengthening trade. On the Russian side, there is an awareness of the limited economic resources as well as scepticism about paying too high a price for integration. Since the Army is weak, the defence budget is shrinking, the organisation is close to a breakdown, and morale is in decay, military means can not be used to force integration.

The second factor preventing the necessary co-operation to develop and explain the "gap" concerns the efforts of the CIS members to strengthen their independence and broaden their contacts with the outside world. With all these states being members of the OSCE, the NACC, the PfP (except Tajikistan), and some members of the Council of Europe, the political map of the former Soviet territory is very different today.

Different regions have developed different degrees of closeness to Russia. The most willing are those most vulnerable and most in need of Russian support. Belarus, Kazakhstan, Kyrgyzstan and Tajikistan fall within this category. Thus the Ukraine, Uzbekistan, Turkmenistan, and Azerbaijan are recognised as the most unwilling – with Ukraine leading the league. Because of internal conflicts, Georgia, Moldova and Armenia are regarded as having to be fairly close although they seem to take the opportunity to opt for more independent policies whenever they can.

As the great power in the region, Russia was successful in preventing a rapid disintegration in 1993. However, there is a grave difference between being successful influencing a region by temporarily securing a basic military-political position as with the Transcaucasus in 1993 and with getting Georgia and Azerbaijan back on track by putting them under pressure during their times of trouble, and by successfully pursuing a policy of voluntary integration. The cases of Georgia and Azerbaijan also illustrate the "power of the weak". Since then, Azerbaijan, despite being a member of both the CIS and the Tashkent Treaty, has followed a comparatively more independent policy whereby Georgian President Shevardnadze has repeatedly demanded a more active mission by the Russian peacekeeping troops deployed along the border of Abkhazia, or withdrawal from the country.

The gap causes frustration and has been used in the domestic power struggle for criticising the Russian president and government.

It has also resulted in harsh and sometimes aggressive statements not only from the Duma Opposition, but also from government officials. Many of these statements seem to have been meant for the domestic debate rather than as serious proposals for policy-making. Such statements create a feeling of insecurity and fear in the outside world concerning Russian intentions. The existence of a gap raises the question of bridging. Theoretically, there are two ways for Moscow to bridge this gap: either by forcing reality to adapt, or by adapting policy to reality.

So far, this gap has had a moderating influence on Russian policy. Concerning integration on CIS territory, Russia has had to adopt a more pragmatic policy. Both in statements by Foreign Minister Primakov and Defence Minister Rodionov, there seems to be a growing and reflected consciousness of Russia's weakness in its policy. The Russia of today would not be capable of forcing its policy on an obstinate reality. What's more, there do not seem to be any politicians within the Kremlin or immediate to the Kremlin who favour such a policy. It is true that the domestic scene might rapidly and drastically change in the event of early presidential elections. Rather, it seems that current circumstances will force Russia to adopt a more pragmatic policy, thereby lowering its ambitions.

The role of the West and Russian Policy

The West is an important factor in Russia's relations with the CIS members. All CIS countries are members of the Organisation for Security and Cooperation in Europe, the North Atlantic Cooperative Council (NACC) and Partnership for Peace (except Tajikistan). Some countries have also become members of the Council of Europe (e.g., Russia and the Ukraine). Western companies are investing capital, and contacts and exchange of all kinds are developing.

These contacts constitute a crucial factor for regional stability and promote, along with other CIS countries, Russian integration in a multilateral European architecture. The involvement of the UN and the OSCE in conflict prevention and resolution in the former Soviet Union is crucial for the creation of a multilateral security organisation for preventing spheres of interest from developing.

The concern of the West is a factor restraining Russian behaviour in relation to the states on the former Soviet territory. The case of the Baltic states is a good illustration. The active engagement of the West in the Baltic states contributed to the peaceful post-Soviet transformation in this area. Besides the Baltic states, Ukraine ranks high on the priority list of concern to the West.

Russia has a dual relation to these organisations. It is a proponent of a multilateral security system with the highest organisations – the UN and the OSCE – as it relates to Central and Eastern Europe, but remains decidedly more sceptical to a 'too large' influence with respect to the former Soviet territory. It has been a strength of Western policy when presenting the UN and OSCE system as the primary model.

The West thus has a restraining effect on Russian policy in the near abroad and may act as a guarantor of stability. According to many in the West, such a function might further develop if military guarantees are extended not only to former Soviet allies, but to former republics as well. However, this policy may have the opposite effect. In spite of all Western declarations that NATO is fundamentally changing in character by taking on peacekeeping tasks, for the Russians it is the security guarantee of Article Five and the possible deployment of conventional as well as nuclear forces in the new NATO member states that matter.

In its current weak state, Russia will probably have to adapt to reality and accept a first "wave" of new NATO members. Still, there is the risk of a negative Russian reaction in a more distant future which should not be underestimated. The elements of a confrontational perspective are already in the making.

The "window of opportunity" for integrating Russia into a multilateral web of relations with the West – including a multilateral security system for Europe – has not been closed yet. The policy of the West is one important factor for Russian foreign policy-making.

Russia and the Baltic States

What conclusions can be drawn from an analysis of Russian policy toward the near abroad with regard for the Baltic states?

Russia has so far not been able to fulfil its objectives concerning the near abroad and thus, for the moment, a gap exists between what reality permits and what actual Russian policy is. The "near abroad" is of highest priority to Russia's foreign and national security policy, yet Moscow still has been forced into a more pragmatic policy far behind its declared ambitions. This can be interpreted as part of an adaption process and can be explained to a large extent by Russia's weakness, resistance from the CIS states, and the factor of Western presence and concern in the area.

Not being members of the CIS or part of the near abroad, the Baltic states are referred to another category. Moscow usually does not use the term "the near abroad" with regard to the Baltic states. However, can they be considered of less concern to Russia?

Officially, Moscow has kept a low profile by avoiding discussions on Russian strategic or military interests in the Baltic states. Yet these states are adjacent to a vulnerable defence district close to the very heart of Russia. Over the centuries, Russia has considered exit to the Baltic Sea a necessity, with consequent conquest or control of the coastline. The discussion of an eventual NATO enlargement to the Baltic states has revealed a deep Russian concern and fear. This was already evident in the May 1992 Draft of the Russian Military Doctrine.

In semi-official statements and political debates there were much more outspoken voices on Russian interests in these states and the "threat" these states might pose to Russia[40] Among those was the by now famous Anton Surikov. In an April 1996 article with Valerii Dementev, he pointed out the strategic position of the Baltic states and their waters.[41] The article is also interesting because of its extreme threat perception of the situation in the Baltic states where "forces of aggressive nationalism supported from the outside and in charge of their own military formations – the army, police and other militarised formations of the Baltic republics" – are mentioned together with the "illegal armed formations of Dudaev, the Tajik Opposition and others". The authors declare that "The Baltic states (Pribaltika) is one of the most explosive regions in regards to the risk of new 'hot beds' of conflicts with the use of Russian military forces". They also mention territorial claims on Russia (including sea territories) by Estonia and Latvia, as well as their eventual integration into NATO.

Official Russian policy has been restrained and has respected laws and decisions by the Baltic governments. This policy has been followed in spite of a strong pressure from the Russian Parliament, which in resolutions has repeatedly urged the government to take hard measures – including economic sanctions against the Baltic states – as an answer to Baltic policy regarding Russian minorities.

During the first years of consensus-building in foreign policy (1993–1994), the much criticised Andrei Kozyrev made remarkably harsh statements concerning the situation of Russians in the Baltic states. Using such terms as "apartheid" and "ethnic cleansing", his words raised the fear in these countries of an eventual turn in Russian policy. His attention-drawing slip of the tongue placing the Baltic states and the near abroad in the same category raised the question of to which degree this was the predominant though unofficial view among Russian military and nationalistic circles.[42]

The harsh Russian media campaign against the Baltic states mainly explains why the popular perception of these states as adversaries to Russia has replaced their early 90s image as forerunners of democracy and close friends to Democratic Russia. As shown by opinion polls from Moscow and Northwest Russia (Sankt Petersburg, Murmansk, Novgorod, Pskov and Kaliningrad), a majority accept military-political measures as a possible Russian reaction against Estonia, Latvia or Lithuania.[43]

Moscow has declared its intention to improve and develop relations with the Baltic states.[44] However, relations remain fairly tense as several practical problems remain to be solved.

The factor of Western presence and concern may remain a good guarantee for stability in the Baltic states during the coming years. However, with Russian policy in the process of pragmatic adaptation, and the Baltic region considered vulnerable to Russian defence, a NATO enlargement may turn out to be counter-productive in regard to the independent Baltic states.

Towards the end of 1996, as a countermove to the preparations for a NATO enlargement decision, official Russian statements sharpened.[45] This included harsh statements from Foreign Minister Primakov concerning the situation of Russian minorities in the Baltic states together with his threats of eventual economic sanctions toward these states.[46]

Still, the conclusion to be drawn so far from Russian policy toward its "near abroad" is that Russia has not resorted to military violence to attain its objectives. Rather, Russia has opted to interfere in the domestic scene by using the vulnerability of these states during times of troubles, and manipulate the scene (as in Georgia and Azerbaijan) in order to put them under pressure and get them back on track within a Russian-dominated Commonwealth.

In terms of the Baltic States' vulnerable national security, the eventual threat from Russia would more likely include the use of political pressure rather than military force or threats. Subsequently, the West's answer to this challenge would be to help minimise all economic and political vulnerabilities of the Baltic states in relation to Russia. However, there can be no remedy for their geographical location i.e., no military guarantees are able to compensate for geography.

Notes

1 Susanne Crow, "Russia Asserts its Strategic Agenda", RFE/RL Research Report, Vol. 2, No. 50, 1993.

2 Alexander Pikayev, "The Russian Domestic Debate on Policy Towards the 'Near Abroad'", in Peacekeeping and the Role of Russia in Eurasia. Edited by Lena Jonson and Clive Archer. (Westview Press 1996).

3 Peacekeeping and the Role of Russia in Eurasia. Eds. Lena Jonson & Clive Archer, Boluder Colorado: Westview Press, 1996.

4 Catherine Dale, The Case of Abkhazia (Georgia)", in Peacekeeping and the Role of Russia in Eurasia; Thomas Golz, "Letter from Eurasia: The Hidden Russian Hand", Foreign Policy, No. 92, Fall 1993.

5 B.D. Porter and C.R. Saivetz, "The Once and Future Empire: Russia and the 'Near Abroad'", in The Washington Quarterly, Summer 1994.

6 See Yeltsin's speech on 28 February 1993 where he laid claim to Russia taking responsibility for maintaining peace and stability in the whole of the former Soviet Union. See Kozyrev's statements during the Autumn of 1993 about Russia not accepting "power vacuums" along its borders to be filled by "other powers, which are not friendly and could even be hostile to Russian interests". (Nezavisimaya Gazeta, 24 November 1993).

7 Voennaya mysl, special issue, May 1992; Krasnaya zvezda, 19 November 1993.

8 In the beginning of July 1995 at a meeting of Russian ambassadors to CIS states, Kozyrev started declaring the CIS a priority to Russian foreign policy. Diplomaticheskii vestnik, 1995, No. 8 (August), pp. 22–26.

9 Decree by the Russian President on Russian Strategy with regard to the Members of the Commonwealth of Independent States. Rossiiskaya gazeta, 23 September 1995.

10 "Doklad Federalnoi Sluzhny Vneshnei Razvedki. Rossiya i SNG: Nuzhdaetsya li v korrektirovke pozitsiya Zapada?", Rossiiskaya gazeta, 22 September 1994, pp. 1 and 6.

11 "Primakov ne schitaet sebya flyugerom", Nezavisimaya gazeta, 13 January 1996, p. 1.

12 Lena Jonson, "Russia and Europe. The Emergence of a New Russian Foreign Policy", in Towards a New European Security Order. (SSIA Stockholm 1996).

13 Lena Jonson, "Russia and European Security: New Wine in Old Bottles?", New Thinking in International Relations: Swedish Perspectives. Edited by Rutger Lindahl and Gunnar Sjöstedt. Stockholm 1995.

14 "Politika natsionalnoi bezopasnosti Rossiiskoi Federatsii (1996–2000)", NG-Stsenarii. Yezhemesyachnoe prilozhenie k "Nezavisimaoi gazete" (May 1996, No. 2). The concept document as well as the long term programme were said to be classified.

15 "Chto ne umestilos v prezidentskoe poslanie", Nezavisimaya gazeta, 28 February 1996.

16 "O natsionalnoi bezopasnosti. Poslanie Prezidenta RF Federalnomu Sobraniyo", Nezavisimaya gazeta, 14 June 1996.

17 Interview with Yevgenii Primakov in Rossiiskaya gazeta, 17 December 1996, "Nasha vneshnyaya politika ne mozhet byt politikoi vtororazryadnogo gosudarstva".

18 One illustration of the new geostrategic trend in Russian debate and perspectives on the world is by Aleksei Gromyko. He claims that Russia still lacks a concept of its national interests. He refers to the Western geopolitical theorist Halford Mackinder from the begininning of this century. Gromyko's admiration for Mackinder may not be shared by wider groups; however, concerning his conclusion regarding the CIS, few would argue with him. "Indisputable is the truth that on the CIS space Russia has geopolitical interests of a strategic character. Efforts to prevent Russia from creating a democratic and mutually beneficial union of CIS members have to be diplomaticcally intersected. Without putting the CIS space in good order, its fragements will become play figures of other world centres". Aleksei Gromyko, "Geopolitika sevodnya i zavtra", Nezavisimaya gazeta, 19 September 1996, p. 5

   Primakov is considered a pragmatic politician in favour of international cooperation. Yet, his worldview is to a large extent dominated by a perspective of rivalry and competition between the leading world powers.

19 Rossiiskaya gazeta 24 February 1994.

20 "Strategiya dlya Rossii I" (Nezavisimaya gazeta, August 1992); and "Strategiya dlya Rossii II" (Nezavisimaya gazeta, 27 May 1994).

21 "Vozroditsya li soyuz? Budushezhee postsovetskogo prostranstva. Tezisy Soveta po vneshnei i oboronnoi politike?, Nezavisimaya gazeta, 23 May 1996.

22 Ukraine has not ratified the Statutes of the CIS.

23 Six states signed the treaty of 15 May 1992. In 1993, Azerbaijan, Georgia and later Belorus joined. Ukraine, Turkmenia and Moldova have not signed the treaty.

24 This was reflected in the 1994 report by the Russian Intelligence Service on Russia and the CIS, where the argument was forwarded that supra-state structures be created by part of the national sovereignty being "delegated".

25 After Shireen T. Hunter, Central Asia Since Independence, The Washington Papers/168, Westport, Connecticut/London, 1996.

26 Decree by the Russian President on Russian strategy with regard to the Members of the Commonwealth of Independent States, Rossiiskaya gazeta, 23 September 1995.

27 An agreeement was signed in 1994. An agreement on exchange of information was signed in 1996 by seven states -Armenia, Belorussia, Moldova, Russia, Tajikistan, Kazakhstan, Kyrgyzstan. "Soglashenie ob obmene informatsiei po voprosam okhrany vneshnikh granits gosudarstv – uchastnikov SNG", Diplomaticheskii vestnik, 1996, No. 5 (May), pp. 34–36.

28 Signed in February 1995 by 10 states (except Azerbaijan and Moldova). A Coordinating Committee on CIS Air Defence was also created. Diplomaticheskii vestnik, 1995, No. 3 (March), p. 31; Izvestiya 10 March 1995; Nezavisimaya gazeta 21 February 1995.

29 In January 1996 a document "Concept on conflict prevention and regulation Adopted by eight of 12 states "Kontseptsiya predotvrasheniya i

uregulirovaniya konfliktov na territorii gosudatstv – uchastnikov SNG", Diplomaticheskii vestnik, 1996, No. 2 (February), pp. 38–42. See also Lena Jonson, In Search of a Doctrine: Russia and Peacekeeping in the CIS. Occasional Papers. Low Intensity Conflict and Law Enforcement (forthcoming).

30 In February 1995 a "Memorandum on Maintaining Peace and Stability in the CIS" was adopted. It was proposed by Nazarbayev and signed by all twelve member states at the Almata summit in February 1995. The signatories declare their intention to prevent the creation and activity of organisations, groups and individuals directed against the independence and territorial integrity of the signatory states by ethnic hatred or external attacks. Special attention was given to the problem of separatism. "Memorandum o podderzhaniyu mira i stabilnosti v SNG", Diplomaticheskii vestnik, 1995, No. 3 (March), pp. 31–33.

A "Concept on Collective Security" was signed by eight member states of the Tashkent Treaty on Collective Security (except Azerbaijan) at the Almata summit in February 1995. Diplomaticheskii vestnik, 1995, No. 3 (March), pp. 33–37. The document gives the principles and tasks of the creation of the collective security system. "Kontseptsiya kollektivnoi bezopasnosti gosudarstv-uchastnikov dogovora". Diplomaticheskii vestnik, 1995, No. 3 (March), pp. 34–36.

31 Agreement on peacekeeping from 1992, see Anna Kreikemeyer & Andrei Zagorsky, "The CIS", Peacekeeping and the Role of Russia in Eurasia. Eds. Lena Jonson & Clive Archer. Boulder, Colo.: Westview Press, 1996. Statutes on peacekeeping troops were adopted at the CIS summit in February 1996 by only six of twelve states "Reshenie ob utverzhdenii Polozheniya o Kollektivnykh silakh po podderzhaniyu mira v SNG", Diplomaticheskii vestnik, 1996, No. 2 (March), pp. 46–52.

32 In April 1994, Yeltsin signed a decree proclaiming Russia's intention to establish 30 military bases on the territory of the former Soviet Union and to be negotiated bilaterally with individual states.

33 BBC Monitoring Service: Former USSR, 22 September 1995; See also the speech by President Yeltsin to the CIS heads of states "Sblizhat nashi strany na osnove partnerstva i vzaimnoi vygody", Rossiiskie vesti 20 January 1996.

34 "On further strenghtening of integration within the economic and humanitarian spheres".

35 Nezavisimaya gazeta, 2 April 1996.

36 Nezavisimaya gazeta, 29 March 1996, pp. 1 and 3.

37 Russian Public Television (ORT), Vremya, 16 May 1996.

38 Nezavisimaya gazeta, 29 March 1996, pp. 1 and 3.

39 See the very critical analysis by Azhdar Kurtov, "Vremya rabotaet ne na integratsiyu", Nezavisimaya gazeta, 25 December 1996, p. 5.

40 See for example Andrannik Migranyan, "Rossiya i blizhnee zarubezhe", Nezavisimaya gazeta, 12 and 18 January 1994, pp. 1, 4, 4–5, 8.

41 Valerii Dementev and Anton Surikov, "Strategiya reformirovaniya vooruzhennykh sil rossiiskoi Federatsii", Nezavisimoe voennoe obozrenie. Prilozhenie k 'Nezavisimoi gazete' No. 7 (11), April 1996.

42 According to Korochenko, journalist at Nezavisimaya gazeta, this view is widespread in these circles.

43 "Rossiya, gosudarstva Baltiiskogo morya i severnoi Evropy: problemy vzaimootnoshenii i budushzhee", (report prepared by the Political Research Fund led by Andrei Federov), Nezavisimaya gazeta 28 May 1996, p. 5.
44 See President Yeltsin's speech on national security in June 1996.
45 See Defence Minister Rodionov to CIS defence ministers, "Igor Rodionov vystupil za sozdanie oboronnogo soyuza stran SNG", Nezavisimaya gazeta, 26 December 1996, p. 1; and the analysis of Primakov's first year as a Foreign Minister, "Pervyi god diplomatii Primakova proshel bez provalov i proryvov", Nezavisimaya gazeta, 9 January 1997, p. 1 ans 2.
46 "Rossiiskaya diplomatiya vybiraet rezkuyu tonalnost", Nezavisimaya gazeta, 11 January 1997, p. 1 and 2.

Chapter 7

Russia and the Baltic States

Challenges and Opportunities

Alexander A. Pikayev

Russo-Baltic Relations: Lessons of History

Russia and the Baltic States of Latvia, Lithuania and Estonia possess a long history of mutual mistrust, wars and close economic and cultural interdependence. The Baltic's geographical situation has caused them to be a zone of contact between Russia and Northern German civilisation. Their territory has been used by Western Europeans as a 'platzdarm' for numerous invasions into Russia's mainland. Conversely, Russia has sought domination in the Baltics in order to consolidate a configuration permitting its further westward movements. Additionally, Moscow, in being isolated from warm-water seas, has attempted to gain access to the Baltic's closest warm-water bays since the late 16th century.

In the 13th century the Teuton warriors invaded Russia from the present day territories of Estonia and Latvia. Their successful invasion and occupation of Pskov, the capital city of North-western Russia's medieval republic, marked the first time a Russian city had ever been occupied by the Germans. It was followed up by the bloody Ice Battle between Alexander Nevsky's troops and the Teutons, a battle which saw the Germans defeated. Though this defeat brought an end to the early medieval 'Drang nach Osten' German crusade, Russian mentality toward the Baltic area since that time has been to consider it as one of the primary sources of aggression from the West.

Four hundred years later the Polish-Lithuanian union 'Rzeczpospolita' invaded deep into Russia's territory and became the first Western state to seize the Russian capital of Moscow. Though Polish-Lithuanian troops were forced to leave Moscow as a result of a national liberation war a few years later, a monument was constructed on the Red Square in the very heart of Moscow for Minin and

Pozharsky, the leaders of the liberation. Today, this symbol still reminds Russians that historically, one of the Baltic states was among its most dangerous rivals.

More recently, during the 1918–1921 Civil War, the territories of Latvia and Estonia were used by the Germans and the Whites from Gen. Yudenich's forces as a starting point for offences directed at the second Russian capital of St. Petersburg.

On numerous occasions, Russia has invaded the Baltic territories as well. Beginning in late 16th century, and again in the early 18th century, the tsars conducted wars aimed at establishing control over port cities situated to the north of the Daugava River. Undertaken even prior to the Moscow state reaching its self-established historic task – to reunite all Russian, Ukrainian and Belarusian lands under Kremlin control – the initial attempt demonstrates how important the mission to gain access to warm-water Baltic Sea ports was for a then rapidly developing Russian trade and commerce.

In the late 18th century after three partitions of Rzechpospolita, all Baltic lands were placed under Russian rule for the first time. This Russian period in Baltic history continued for two hundred years until the crash of the Russian Empire in 1917, and of the Kaiser Reich in 1918 opened the doors for Baltic independence. Unfortunately, this period lasted just twenty years. In the 1920s and 1930s, the inability of Western nations to include the Soviet Union and Weimar Germany into the larger European security system refuelled revisionist feelings in Moscow and Berlin. British and French attempts to channel German aggression to the East forced the USSR into agreements with Berlin concerning the provisional settlement of Eastern Europe, agreements which included defining the spheres of influence. According to Soviet historiography, the 1939 Molotov-Ribbentrop Accords incorporating the Baltic States into the Soviet Union were almost unanimously described as an attempt to move the expected Soviet-German front-line as far from Moscow and Leningrad as possible.

This brief historic description of Russo-Baltic relations highlights one paradox: Russia and the Baltic States have never had wars between them. Even the Baltic's incorporation into the USSR in 1939–40 was not a consequence of formal war. Unlike Finland's experience in demonstrating that the Soviet military machine could be effectively stopped by a much weaker defender, the Balts preferred not to defend their independence with arms.

History has taught the Russians that when Baltic territories come under the dominance of an outside power such as the Germans, Poles or Swedes, it inevitably becomes a source of invasion against Russia. Conversely, rare periods of peace between Russia and the Balts have coincided with periods where nothing from the Baltic territories has threatened Russian lands. This, in fact, has proved to be the case when the Balts have enjoyed de jure or de facto independence from the outside world.

Prior to the German (and Danish) 12th century crusades, Baltic tribes were able to successfully maintain independence from the huge cradle of the Russian state, the Kiev Great Princedom. This Princedom limited itself by establishing control over peripheral areas such as Latgalia (now eastern Latvia) and South-eastern Estonia (where the city of Yuriev – now Tartu – was founded). The Kiev princes never had the task of occupying the entire Baltic territory. In turn, they tended to consider it not as a gate to the Western world, but as a barrier preventing the West from invading the Great Princedom possessions.

Additionally, up until the 14th century, main trade routes circumvented Baltic lands. Trade caravans moved along the Dnie-per-Volkhov-Neva waterway. Transit values for the Balts emerged later on when Germans and Danes established ports such as Riga and Revel. Their effect radically improved the Baltic infrastructure and provided a much higher territorial integrity than what was previously the case among the numerous local tribes.

Since the 16th century, Russia's emerging economy has been so heavily dependent upon access to Baltic ports that over a span of 150 years, Moscow tsars never abandoned their attempts to seize Livonia. The Swedish occupation of Ingria – presently the St. Petersburg area – in the early 17th century denied Russia its limited historical access via the Neva waterway to the frozen Finnish Gulf. This move forced Moscow to reach another conclusion: those who controlled Livonia could one day completely deny Russia its traditional export routes to the Baltic Sea. Subsequently, it provoked Moscow to make a more concerted effort not only to remove the Swedes from the Neva estuary, but to acquire the remaining Baltic area (then controlled from Stockholm) as a pre-emptive measure against future Swedish (and others) revanche.

From this, the second lesson was learned: as long as Russia was denied access to warm-water ports to the north from the river of Daugava (or Western Dvina), it would never cease its attempts to penetrate the geopolitical barrier separating it from the open Baltic Sea. Even the weak, 17th century post-invasion Russia, on several occasions, attempted to regain its former control over Ingria. And as it grew stronger under Peter the Great, its recapture of the Neva estuary did not cease at the banks of Narova River. Sweden's entire Baltic occupation was overthrown in order to provide Moscow with reliable access to the open Baltic Sea as well as to prevent future Swedish or other Western penetration via Daugava to the north.

Between World War I and World War II, the Baltic States' participation in the anti-Soviet 'cordon sanitaire', together with their solemn orientation towards London and Paris, did not provide them with reliable security guarantees. The Versailles pattern of European security, aimed at keeping Germany and the Soviet Union out, did not survive its 21st anniversary. As a result, the Balts again became a hostage of Russo-German relations; in 1941–45, their territories were transformed into a Russian-German battlefield.

This then leads to the third lesson: in the long run, Baltic security cannot be seen as reliable or sustainable without Russia. Exceptional reliance on Western powers would inevitably invoke Moscow's worst historical syndromes of the Ice Battle and the Polish-Lithuanian seizure of the Kremlin. Consequently, Russia would do everything in its power to deny Western troop deployments on Baltic soil; and similar to the 16th–18th centuries, it would never abandon its attempts to use every opportunity for gaining control over the Baltic lands.

Perhaps fittingly then, the Soviet Baltic republics' struggle for independence in 1989–91 gained limited international support. Numerous appeals on the part of Baltic politicians fell empty as no one in the West wanted to jeopardise relations with Moscow by recognising the Baltic independence unilaterally. Only President Yeltsin's August 1991 decrees proclaiming a new Russia's recognition of the independence of Latvia, Lithuania and Estonia, opened the way for not only de facto, but de jure international recognition of independence.

And herein lies the fourth lesson: the Baltic States were able to reinstitute their independence only as a result of a democratic revolution in Russia. Therefore, maintaining democracy in Russia represents the best assurance for the Baltics' future independence.

Since the 18th century, the Baltic and Russian economies have become deeply interwoven. By the late 19th century, Riga had become one of Russia's ten biggest industrial centres. At the same time Libava (now Liepaja), after constructing a railway from Russia's agricultural heartland, transformed itself into the largest port exporting Russian grain. Later, the World War I interruption of economic ties with the Soviet Union led to a significant degradation of Latvian urban centres.

During the inter-war period the population of Liepaja decreased so dramatically that it never reached its 1914 peak again. The Baltic economies generally became de-industrialized. Being largely dependent upon agricultural export to the West, their economies suffered deeply when the world markets collapsed during the Great Depression of the 1930s. Domestic instability ensued. Taken together, this perhaps provides an explanation as to why the Baltic societies – contrary to Finland's – became so vulnerable to Soviet pressures of 1939–40.

Thus, the fifth lesson: economic ties with Russia represent another guarantee for Baltic independence because they provide a natural source for an economic recovery i.e., a stronger economy would help to consolidate domestic stability and, therefore, independence.

In sum, Russian-Baltic history provides five lessons for their on-going relations:

1 Every time a Baltic territory emerges under the dominance of a Western power, it becomes a platzdarm for invasion of Russia's mainland; alternatively, Baltic independence (or autonomy) coincides with periods of generally peaceful Russo-Baltic relations;
2 Russia's isolation from warm-water Baltic ports always invites Moscow's aggressions into the Baltic territories;
3 Without Russian participation, Baltic security can never be viewed as reliable or sustainable;
4 Democracy in Russia represents a main source for modern Baltic independence and provides important security guarantees in and of itself;
5 Interruption of economic co-operation with Russia would necessarily undermine Baltic economies and their domestic stability.

In more general terms, the Baltic States occupy a unique geopolitical position vis-à-vis Russia, and between Russia and the West. Historically, they have been a gate for both Western aggressions against Russia, and Russian invasions against the West. Too often, they have been used as a front-line between Russian and Western worlds. The question invoked today is whether the paradigm of the past will survive, or whether the Baltic States can find an alternative option for connecting the two historic rivals together.

Conflicting rationale of Russo-Baltic relations

The Baltic States belong to the smallest of European nations. Latvia and Estonia occupy territories that are among the dozen least populated European states[1]. The combined population of the Baltic States – not even eight million people – is less than the population of Moscow. Not surprisingly, therefore, Riga, Tallinn and Vilnius feel uncomfortable in the shadow of the huge Russian elephant.

Vis-à-vis Latvia and, in particular, Estonia, Russia proves to be a much poorer neighbour. Per capita living standards in the two Baltic states are on average almost twice as high as in Russia. Given that Russia's relative wealth is concentrated to a few oblasts and cities such as Moscow, Tyumen, Nizhny Novgorod, Yekaterinburg, etc., the gap between Estonia and Latvia on the one hand, and Russia's border oblasts of Pskov and Leningrad on the other, looms even larger.

Russia's predominance, together with the poverty of its borderland, has created pressures of a different kind. Higher living standards in the Baltic States attract poor border area populations eager to find better paying jobs. Geographically positioned between Russia and the Scandinavian countries, the Baltic States are often used as a transit corridor by illegal Asian and African immigrants on their way from Russia to Sweden. Additionally, should Russia's domestic stability fail, the Baltic States can expect a tremendous influx of refugees of Russian origin.

As shown in Table 1, Russian military capabilities prevail over those of the Baltic States by a considerable margin. In 1995, the personnel of Russia's ground forces located in areas having a common border with the Baltic States – the North-western Military District (MD) and Kaliningrad oblast' – was 12 times higher than the ground forces of Estonia, Latvia, and Lithuania put together. Neither of the three Baltic States possessed combat aircraft or battle tanks, nor any real air

Table 1. Comparison of Russian troops deployed in North-western Military District and Kaliningrad Oblast with Aggregate Size of Armed Forces of Estonia, Latvia and Lithuania (1995)[2]

Type of Capabilities	North-western MD and Kaliningrad Oblast'	Baltic States	Comparison
Personnel (ground)	111,000	9,100	12.2:1
Tanks	1,820	NO	
Armoured Combat Vehicles	2,580	87	29.7:1
Artillery	1,410	75	18,8:1
Combat aircraft	437	NO	–
Attack helicopters	132	9	14,7:1

Source: The Military Balance 1995/96, pp. 84–85, 89–90, 118–119.

defence capabilities. In such categories as armoured combat vehicles and helicopters, their gaps were estimated at 15–30 to one. The overall size of Latvian ground forces amounted to 1,500 men. Combined with the absence of a national air defence, this meant that even a single undermanned Russian airborne troop division located in Pskov could theoretically size up key Latvian facilities within a few hours.

Aside from this objective controversy in Russian-Baltic relations, the two sides have been further complicated by purely emotional prejudices. In the eyes of the Lithuanians, Latvians and Estonians, Russians remain the occupants who destroyed their independence. Since 1940, Russian rule has been accompanied by repressions which have touched almost every Baltic family. The Soviet economic management turned out to be so inefficient that in the 1970s and 1980s, despite being traditional agricultural exporters, the Baltic republics faced food shortages. The Balts also blame Moscow for their inability to secure economic growth. They have repeatedly pointed out that during the Soviet period of their history, the economic gap with such neighbouring states as Finland increased dramatically.

During recent years, one can observe a growing prejudice toward the Balts from the Russian side as well. Mistreatment of Russian minorities in Latvia and Estonia, territorial claims to Russia on the part of the Balts, as well as active participation in illegal trafficking of arms into Russia, and raw materials out of the country has led to the paradoxical situation where it is almost impossible to find a friendly attitude among the Russian elite even though this very elite, in 1989–91, supported the Baltic struggle for independence and made it a political reality.

Like other countries of Central Europe, the Baltic States perceive themselves culturally and politically to be inseparable from, and an integral part of, Europe. Therefore, their chief strategic foreign policy initiative is integration into the community of developed Western nations. The once poor and unstable Southern European states of Greece and Portugal, which gained political stability and economic growth through participation in the European Union, stands as an especially attractive example for the Balts. The Baltic States realise the need for Western investments as the source of their economic recovery just as they surely know Western markets are the key to increasing their exports.

As a result of an open door policy to the West, the European Union's share in Baltic foreign trade since the Soviet's disintegration has increased significantly. In 1991, slightly more than two percent of

Estonia's imports and exports were traded with Finland. By 1995, this figure reached 35.7 percent of Estonian import, and 20.9 of its export[3]. In the same year, Latvia imported 49 percent of its goods and services from the European Union while the EU's share in Lithuanian imports reached 40 percent[4].

The Baltic States have remain interested in Eastern markets as well. Similar to their Soviet period, warm-water ports are widely used by Russian exporters. In fact, Russian transit provides the single largest source of hard currency income both for Estonia and, in particular, Latvia. The latter is connected by a pipeline with Russian oil-producing areas and possesses the largest oil exporting terminal at Ventspils (Western Latvia, Kurzeme). Russian oil is delivered by railway to the main Lithuanian port – Klaipeda. Tallinn mainly specialises in bulk commodities coming from Russia. Ports of all three states are also used for importing grain into Russia.

The significance of this transit for the Baltic States can be illustrated by estimates from the Russian Foreign Ministry. According to their estimates, Russian transit through Estonia reaches 12 million tons, or roughly 300 million dollars annually[5]. This figure equals approximately 10 percent of Estonian GDP.

However, uneasy political relationships have affected the transit relationship as well. Growing Russian imports and exports implies looking for alternatives in order to lower trade dependence on foreign ports. Russia's slow but steadily progressing construction of new port facilities on its own coast, such as the facility under construction half way between St. Petersburg and Estonian border in Ust-Luga, offer an example. During recent years, even the role of Finland's geographically less desirable port facilities (vis-à-vis Russia's heartland) has increased.

In spite of all attempts to diversify the sources of energy deliveries, the Baltic States' energy consumption remains almost completely dependent on deliveries of Russian oil and gas. Furthermore, Lithuania needs Russian disposal facilities for disposing spent fuel from its Ignalina nuclear power plant.

The Baltic States face certain complications in utilising the huge Russian market for industrial export. In times of economic difficulty, Russian consumers traditionally have problems paying the price required by Baltic producers for Baltic goods. The Riga Railcar Producing Plant (RVZ), once a virtual monopoly in the USSR, almost lost the market because Russian railways were unable to pay the greatly increased prices. Instead, the Russian Transportation Ministry launched a program aimed at the construction of railcars on Russian railcar maintenance facilities (in Torzhok, Voronezh, etc.,).

Furthermore, Baltic goods now face tougher competition from better quality Western commodities. As an example, the RAF Car Plant in Yelgava (located 90 kilometres south of Riga and another former Soviet monopolist), responsing to the liberalisation of imports after the Soviet collapse needed to greatly reduce its deliveries of minivans to Russia despite the absence of any Russian domestic minivan production. This was largely due to the influx of much better quality, and only slightly higher priced Western and Japanese minivans. The problem facing the Baltics in this regard is that due to their complicated political relationship with Russia, it has been refused the preferential tariffs allotted to other former Soviet republics. As a result, Baltic goods in Russian market prices have almost reached those of their Western counterparts; given their lower quality, this has undermined their competitiveness.

The above mentioned economic and political problems have reduced Russia's share of the foreign trade balances of all three Baltic states. In 1991, 45.9 percent of Estonian imports came from Russia. In 1995, this figure decreased to 15.6 percent. Developments in Latvia and Lithuania show the same trend (though their Russian shares remain higher[6]). Nevertheless, in terms of absolute size, Russo-Baltic trade has increased significantly According to official Russian statistics for the years 1992–95, Russia's trade balance with the three Baltic states increased more than three-fold from slightly more than 1 billion US dollars to 3.3 billion US dollars[7]. This statistical paradox can be partially explained by the growing re-export of Russian energy resources and non-ferrous metals to the West. It is included in the statistics twice: once under the category of "imports from Russia", and another from the category of "exports from the Baltic States to the West".

In the case of Latvia and Estonia, their Soviet periods led to a considerable increase in the proportion of populations not of indigenous origin. According to the last Soviet census (conducted in 1989), upwards of 48 percent of the Latvian population and 40 percent of the Estonian population were represented by Russian-speaking minorities. In Riga the number of non-Latvian residents far exceeded one out of every two, and in Latvia's second largest city of Daugavpils (Dvinsk), Russian-speaking persons numbered more than 80%. Though the non-indigenous population still represents a high share, recent official Latvian and Estonian statistics show much lower figures – two-fifths for Latvia and roughly one-third for Estonia.

Naturally the Balts see the present high proportion of national minorities as being the result of a Soviet Russification policy, reminding them that as recently as 1935 (at least in Latvia's case), Russians, Ukrainians and Belarusians constituted only 10.3 percent of the country's population[8]. Consequently, they perceive the presence of strong national minorities mainly of Russian and Russian-related origin as being a challenge for the Baltic's national identities.

In order to preserve this, Latvia and Estonia have adopted very restrictive procedures for granting citizenship to Russian-speakers. The 1994 Law on Citizenship (adopted by Latvia on July 22 of that year) automatically provided Latvian citizenship to citizens of the Latvian Republic (and their descendants) as of June 17, 1940[9]. As a consequence, almost 700,000 people (equal to almost 30 percent of the country's population) – most of whom were Russian-speaking – became non-citizens. Those who were born outside Latvia, but lived there for a period of no less than five years dating from 1990, have the right to ask for naturalisation – but only after the year 2000. Conversely, since 1996 those who were born inside Latvia can already ask for naturalisation. Due to procedural difficulties, however, only 3,100 persons have received their citizenship from February 1995 until the end of 1996. In fact, only 450 out of the 33,000 persons eligible for naturalisation in 1996 applied[10].

Incidentally, the 1994 Citizenship Law contradicts the basic principle of the 1919 Citizenship Law, which offered Latvian citizenship to all former citizens of the Russian state who lived in, or were associated with the territory which became Latvia, and who had not previously adopted other citizenship[11].

According to the 1994 Law, non-citizens who served in foreign armed forces could not apply for Latvian naturalisation. This paved the way for denial of citizenship to everyone who passed draft service in the Soviet army, with the exception of pre-1940 Latvian citizens and their descendants[12]. Since military service is obligatory for all young Soviet males, the vast majority of Russian-speaking men in Latvia cannot expect to receive citizenship – including those who were born in Latvia and have lived there 50 years. Links with "occupational armed forces" also prevents the registration of more than 100,000 people listed as alien residents in Latvia, and ultimately poses the risk of deportation from the country.

After five years of independence, it has become clear that these restrictive citizenship rules have not re-ignited Russian-speakers' mass repatriation into the CIS. Since 1990, exodus of the Russian population from Latvia is estimated at 120,000 (with the peak year being 1992 when a majority of Russian military personnel and their families left the country). Since that time, emigration has gradually declined and almost come to a halt by 1996[13]. According to Russian statistics for the years 1992–95, approximately 200,000 immigrants arrived to Russia from the Baltic States: 58,000 from Estonia, 95,000 from Latvia, and 48,000 from Lithuania. In 1996, Russian data also shows significant reduction in newly arrived repatriates[14]. Presumably, a majority of Russian-speakers preferred to stay in Latvia and Estonia because they faced the possibility of much lower standards of living in Russia, especially in the Ukraine and Belarus.

However, a country where approximately one-quarter to one-third of the population is left without realistic hopes for citizenship during their lifetime does seem quite explosive. It would appear that the inability of Latvia and Estonia to incorporate a majority of Russian-speakers into their societies will represent a growing and much more serious challenge to their domestic integrity than would the high percentage of those people. As the 1960s experience of a much more economically prosperous United States shows, a civil rights movement could, at some point, become highly painful for a country's domestic stability.

Contrary to what occurred in Latvia, difficulties in receiving local citizenship forced many Russian-speaking people in Estonia to apply for Russian citizenship. By 1995–96, this process had accelerated. In fact, by October 1, 1996, 110,000 Estonian inhabitants became Russian citizens, while another 113,800 residents in Estonia applied for an alien passport[15]. There can be little doubt that in a country where almost 10 percent of its population is represented by foreign citizens – specifically citizens from a neighbouring state where borders have not been demarcated yet – serious challenges are expected for the integrity of Estonian society.

Restrictive citizenship legislation in Latvia and Estonia violates the agreements signed with Russia in early 1991, where Riga and Tallinn obliged to provide local citizenship for all residents living on their territory. Those agreements represented important elements of a legal base for Latvian and Estonian independence and, as such, were an inseparable part of a package guaranteeing Russia's recognition of their independence. Without these agreements, even Yeltsin's 1991

Russia would have had great difficulty recognising the Baltics' independence, a scenario which could have effectively prevented wider international recognition.

Not surprisingly, this situation aggravates Russian relations with Estonia and Latvia. The Kremlin has grounds to believe that in 1991, Baltic leaders simply deceived them by too easily making what now appears to be empty promises. In Russia's eyes, it must devalue the significance of potential results reached in Russo-Baltic negotiations because they may simply be ignored by the Baltic leaders.

The 1991 agreements provide Russia with the necessary legal base to ask Estonia and Latvia to fulfil their international obligations. The Kremlin consistently directs the attention of Estonian and Latvian leaders, as well as the international community, to the poor state of civil rights in those countries. The latest document, adopted in February 1997 by President Yeltsin and titled "Long-term Line of Russia Towards the Baltic States", states: "Defending compatriots' rights in Baltic States . . . [is] a long-term task of Russia's foreign policy in the region. Among our priorities – establishing, through bilateral dialogue, conditions for providing citizenship for all Russian-speaking inhabitants of Estonia and Latvia, for those who possessed permanent registration there by the time of proclaiming their independence, facilitating procedure of naturalisation, providing right of citizenship based on a fact of birth and families' reunification, halting discrimination of orthodox believers in Estonia. This is our position based on European human rights standards and has nothing in common with interfering into internal affairs of the Baltic States."[16].

It should be mentioned that the Kremlin's objections on the human rights situation in Estonia and Latvia have always been delivered in a manner fully consistent with international law. Moscow initiated or supported consideration of the question in various international forums such as the United Nations, the OSCE and the Council of Europe (which possesses a mandate on monitoring human rights conditions in the member states). Russia has never used the human rights question as a pretext for launching subversive actions against the Balts, or for promoting separatist trends in Russian-populated areas. Moscow has never attempted to use force – or threatened the use of force – in order to solve the minority problem. Despite some internal debates, it has also avoided imposing economic sanctions against Latvia and Estonia, a measure frequently and unilaterally employed by the United States for achieving their foreign policy tasks.

Since 1991, Russia's self restraint has become an important – if not vital – factor for maintaining the stability of Baltic societies and their successful nation building.

Another serious irritation in Russo-Baltic relations is represented by Baltic territorial claims to Russia. Estonia officially claims Russian territories located to the west from the 1939 Soviet-Estonian border, established by the 1921 Tartu Peace Treaty. After Estonian incorporation into the Soviet Union, the border between the Russian Federation and Estonia was moved westward by the Soviet authorities. The disputed territory consists of a belt located along the right bank of a river of Narova within the city of Ivangorod; to the south-east it includes so called 'Eastern Setumaa' where the old Russian town of Izborsk and the Pechory monastery are located.

The predominant Russian population lives in those areas. Historically, a major portion has belonged to the medieval republics of Pskov and Novgorod (later, they were incorporated into the Moscow state). Ivangorod was established by tsar Ivan Grozny in the late 16th century and, since that time (with the exception of some interruptions in the 17th century), it belonged to Russia up until 1918. The Eastern Setumaa hosts the ancient Pechory monastery, Moscow Patriarchy's second most important monastery after Troitse-Sergieva Lavra (this has also always belonged to Russia until 1918).

In September 1996 during the Petrozavodsk meeting of the Council of the Baltic Sea States, Estonia hinted that it was ready to withdraw its territorial claims to Russia and conclude a border demarcation agreement as soon as possible. This represented an important shift in Tallinn diplomacy, which earlier bluntly rejected the very opportunity to abandon border claims before Russia recognised validity of the 1921 Tartu Peace Treaty. After Petrozavodsk, however, Estonia continued to insist on the necessity of Russia's recognition of the Tartu Treaty. This can be interpreted that Tallinn, while abandoning explicit territorial claims, still maintained them implicitly by the act of asking Moscow to recognise the Treaty which established a legal base for the 1921–1940 Soviet-Estonian border.

In 1996, the Latvian Parliament adopted a resolution claiming the pre-war Abrene county territory (currently the Pytalovo region of the Pskov oblast). Despite this resolution, the Latvian government officially refrained from raising the issue during the Russian-Latvian negotiations. In February 1997, the Latvian Ministry of Foreign Affairs rejected the allegations contained in the "Russian Presidential

Long-Term Line Towards the Baltic States" on Latvian territorial claims and emphasised its readiness to solve the issue of the Russian-Latvian border demarcation constructively, and in accordance with international law[17].

Ironically, Estonia and Latvia, by claiming the transfer of certain territories during the Soviet occupation to be illegal, placed the third Baltic State – Lithuania – in a difficult position because many important Lithuanian territories like the capital city of Vilnius and the major port Klaipeda (Memel) were incorporated into modern Lithuania precisely during the period of the Soviet occupation. Under the Molotov-Ribbentrop accords, Vilnius was returned to Lithuania by Moscow in 1939 after the Russian-German partition of Poland. Incorporation of Klaipeda became possible after World War II, when the Soviet Union gained Eastern Prussia as a result of the post-war settlement in Europe.

Officially, Lithuania has never raised territorial claims to Russia. Nevertheless, some Lithuanian politicians refer to the Russian Kaliningrad oblast' (which in early medieval times belonged to Lithuania) as a 'small Lithuania'. In March 1992, Lithuanian Ambassador to the United States Stasis Lozoriatis said that the Kaliningrad oblast' would one day be a part of Lithuania. In February 1995 Lithuanian Parliament member Ozolas stated that Europe must reconsider Kaliningrad oblast' status and unequivocally determine to whom it legally belongs[18].

The 1991–1996 territorial problems in Russian-Estonian and, to a lesser extent, Russian-Latvian relations not only complicated relations between the countries, but, ultimately, could produce more problems for Estonia and Latvia in the foreseeable future. Absence of bilaterally recognised Russian borders seem particularly risky for Tallinn and Riga, whose own border lands (like the city of Narva) possess large Russian majorities.

Issues concerning Russian minorities and Baltic territorial claims affect Russia's domestic political scene as well. In 1991–93, the perceived mistreatment of ethnic Russians in Latvia and Estonia became a beloved argument for the Communist opposition to President Yeltsin. It also provoked an increase of xenophobic and ultra-nationalistic sentiments in such border areas as the Pskov oblast. During the 1996 elections for local governor, a majority of the voters chose a candidate from Vladimir Zhirinovsky's ultra-nationalist Liberal Democratic party. Nowhere else did the Party's representatives gain such success.

Russian-Baltic and, in particular, Russian-Lithuanian relations are complicated by the problem of Kaliningrad. This exclave, being separated from mainland Russia by Lithuanian and Belarusian territories, occupies a unique position in modern Europe. Kaliningrad hosts the headquarters of the Baltic fleet and also remains Russia's only large, warm-water port on the Baltic coast. There are approximately 40,000 troops deployed in the exclave.

The transit issue has economic, political and military dimensions. Economically for Russia's export goods, Kaliningrad competes with Lithuanian port of Klaipeda. In order to induce Russian exporters to use Klaipeda, Lithuania has established preferential transit fees for Klaipeda, and higher transit tariffs for Kaliningrad. This has seriously damaged the economy of the exclave.

The presence of Russian troops in the Kaliningrad area is often cited by Baltic, Polish and German politicians to demonstrate that the "Russian threat" is still alive in the Baltic area. On February 16, 1994 the European Parliament adopted a resolution underlining the necessity for urgent troops withdrawals from the oblast' and the reduction in size of Russian forces deployed to a level of reasonable sufficiency. On November 13, 1994 the Baltic Assembly passed a resolution asking to organise an international meeting regarding the demilitarisation of the Kaliningrad oblast'. On April 19, 1995 a draft resolution was submitted for consideration by the US Congress. It called for the oblast' demilitarisation and the establishment of an international administration in Kaliningrad[19].

An analysis of real force deployments does not confirm claims on militarization of the exclave. According to data of the International Institute of Strategic Studies (see Table 2), in the period from 1990–1995, a bulk of major conventional forces categories deployed there had been reduced. Among the reduced categories were: a number of personnel armoured combat vehicles (reduced by 10 percent); artillery (by 40 percent); and combat aircrafts (by more than three-fold). Only the number of tanks and helicopters increased slightly (by 8 percent in each category)[20].

Russian military deployments in Kaliningrad are in full compliance with the 1991 Paris Treaty on limiting conventional forces in Europe (CFE Treaty). Moreover, Russia maintains a military presence there at much lower levels than those permitted by the Treaty. In order to meet the CFE levels, Moscow has the right to additionally deploy more than 200 tanks, 300 pieces of artillery, and more than 5000 armoured combat vehicles (see Table 2) in the exclave. The Treaty does not

Table 2. Russian Forces Deployed in Kaliningrad

Forces	1990	1995	CFE Ceilings for Kaliningrad
Manpower	60,000(a)	40,000	1,450,000(b)
Tanks	802	870	1,100
Armoured Combat Vehicles	1,081	980	6,060
Artillery	677	410	735
Attack Helicopters	48	52	3,450(b)
Combat Aircraft	155	42	890(b)

(a) in 1992, including Border Troops;
(b) There is no limits for the CFE Subzone IV.3. Restrictions apply for the whole ATTU area, i.e., all European Russia.
Sources: Military Balance 1995/96, pp. 105, 118, 298. Leonid Vardomsky, Lyudmila Vorobyova, Aleksandr Yershov, Kaliningradskaia oblast' Rossiiskoi Federatsii: problemy i perspektivy (Kaliningrad Oblast' of the Russian Federation: Problems and Prospects). – Chapter in: Kaliningradskaia oblast' segodnya, zavtra (Kaliningrad Oblast' – Today, Tomorrow), Research Reports of Moscow Carnegie Center, Issue Fifth, Carnegie Endowment for International Peace, M., Raduga Publishing House, 1995, p. 36.

establish specific ceilings on combat aircraft, attack helicopters and manpower in the area (which if necessary, opens the way for their significant enforcement).

Artificially high limits for Kaliningrad are the result of the fact that the CFE Treaty became obsolete even before it entered into force and was negotiated within the context of the NATO/Warsaw Pact conventional balance in Europe. However, in 1990 – a year before the Treaty was signed in Paris – that balance, together with Warsaw Pact, ceased to exist. Then, in December 1991, the Soviet Union itself disintegrated. These developments led to the rapidly ,changing rationale during intra-former Warsaw Pact negotiations on distributing quotas imposed by the CFE.

The Kaliningrad area was part of an extended central zone (subzone IV.3) of the Treaty to which certain restrictions were applied. It also included Poland, Hungary, Czechoslovakia, Baltic, Carpathian, Kiev and Belarusian military districts of the Soviet Union as well. Countries located in this zone have to agree amongst themselves as to how they would apportion permitted allocations of conventional arms in the area. In 1990, such negotiations took place between the USSR and its three former Central European allies. Due in principle to an already agreed upon Soviet troop withdrawal, along with the new nature of relations with the West, the Central Europeans agreed on low quotas for themselves. The Soviet side perceived the apportionment profitable because it permitted the USSR to concentrate more troops along the Soviet Western border, a position necessary for building up a new forward echelon of defence.

In 1991, the newly independent Baltic States refused to become parties of the CFE Treaty on the grounds that in 1940, they were illegally incorporated into the Soviet Union and thus not considered as Soviet successor states vis-à-vis the Treaty. It was a good decision for Moscow because it helped it maintain control over the whole quota negotiated for the Soviet Union for subzone IV.3. In retrospect, this Baltic decision seems short-sighted because the Balts lost opportunity to reduce Russian permitted deployments in Kaliningrad.

After the Soviet collapse, the Kaliningrad area became the only Russian territory located in the extended central zone. Due to the Baltic's self-abstention in 1992, negotiations on apportioning the Soviet quota between Russia, Ukraine and Belarus commenced. Despite large Russian concessions for the Ukraine, Kiev and Minsk were not able to negotiate such high ceilings that would deprive Russian deployments in the zone[21]. However, limits agreed for Belarus on some categories e.g., tanks, armoured combat vehicles, artillery, outnumbered ceilings imposed two years prior for the much bigger Poland[22].

The problem of high Russian ceilings for Kaliningrad could be solved if the West would adopt a more conciliatory position on the CFE adaptation to the new post-Soviet realities after 1992. However, as late as 1997 the West responded negatively.

Possible Russian decisions concerning unilateral force reductions in Kaliningrad were affected by a chain of provocative statements raised by various Baltic and Western institutions and politicians over the necessity to change the status of the exclave. In the above mentioned 1994 resolution, the European Parliament mentioned that the oblast – but not Russia as a whole – was associated with Europe, thus implicitly raising the question of the oblast's status vis-à-vis the Russian Federation. During his visit to Lithuania in April 1995, German Foreign Minister Kinkel, together with the Baltic States, stated that the exclave – again, not Russia – must become an inseparable part of Europe. Certain German, Polish and Lithuanian politicians openly raised claims on the area. Others adopted provocative statements of a different kind. The Baltic Assembly in its 1994 resolution asked that Kaliningrad's locations be returned to their historical names[23] (before 1919, some of the Baltic cities had

Russian names such as Yuriev (Tartu), Dvinsk (Daugavpils), Rezhitsa (Rezekne), etc.). That resolution today seems counterproductive for Baltic sustainability.

Poles often mention their desire to enter NATO as a need to become part of Europe. But together with the Kaliningrad statements from the German foreign minister, Russia's suspicions about real Western intentions towards the exclave can only increase, subsequently producing motivations to maintain a strong military presence there. From the viewpoint of Russian military planners, forces in Kaliningrad must be sufficient enough to prevent quick occupation by any foreign nation.

In this respect, Moscow would tend to balance force deployments in Kaliningrad not with Lithuania, but with Poland (see Table 3). A comparison of the balance between Kaliningrad and Poland shows that what is perceived in Lithuania as overmilitarization of the oblast, can in Russia be evaluated as insufficient deployments in a vulnerable theatre of potential military operations.

Poland enjoys predominance in all conventional arms and manpower categories. It is decisive in such key categories as manpower and combat aircraft. Militarily, this indicates that Warsaw's fears regarding Kaliningrad's militarization are absolutely groundless. The Kaliningrad group of forces is too weak to launch any offensive against Poland. Conversely, Poland possesses sufficient military predominance to launch a successful offensive operation against the exclave.

In the current political environment, however, it would be extremely difficult to imagine a war in the South-eastern Baltics as the result of a Polish offensive against Kaliningrad. But from Moscow's standpoint, it is equally difficult to imagine a Russian aggression against Lithuania as well. At a time when Russia is

Table 3. Russian-Polish Military Balance Around Kaliningrad

Type of Forces	Kaliningrad	Poland	Ratio
Manpower (ground)	24,000	188,200	1:7,8
Tanks	870	2,017	1:2,3
Armoured Combat Vehicles	980	1,590	1:1,6
Artillery	410	1,879	1:4,6
Attack Helicopters	52	80	1:1,5
Combat Aircraft	32	412	1:12,9

Source: Military Balance 1995/96, pp. 118, 298.

economically so dependent on the West, such a move must be deemed too risky. From a purely military viewpoint, such aggressive action under the existing military balance would expose Kaliningrad to the possibility of counter Polish actions against the rear offending forces.

Poland's predominance in the Polish/Russian military balance in Kaliningrad does not automatically equate to an aggressiveness on the part of Warsaw. Similarly, the same conclusion should be expanded to include Russia as well. Russia's predominance over the Baltic States, created by natural differences in the countries' sizes, should not automatically be interpreted as a natural desire to occupy them.

Since 1994 the Baltic States have initiated a vigorous campaign aimed at incorporation into NATO. In their eyes, such inclusion into the Western community of nations would be irreversible, and thus reliably protect them from possible Russian aggression. The Balts have pointed out that their neutrality did not save them from Soviet occupation in 1940[24]. They also believe their small size does not permit the creation of military capabilities sufficient enough to deter Russia.

This last point is debatable, however. Neighbouring, non-allied Finland, with a population (5.1 million people) less than the total population of the three Baltic States, was able to establish credible defences that proved sufficient against the present size of Russian troops located in the North-western military district (see Table 4). Certainly, Russia's NWMD enjoys a predominance over Finland in the majority of listed categories of conventional weapons. But this predominance is far less than, say, Poland's predominance over the Kaliningrad group of forces. What is even more significant is the fact that Finland possesses very large numbers of artillery and, taken together with its developed air defence, effectively neutralises its inferiority in the number of aircrafts and tanks. Given this standing, and the fact that NWMD troops are not able to concentrate entirely

Table 4. Military Balance Between Finland and Russia's North-western Military District

Type of Forces	NWMD	Finland	Ratio
Manpower (ground)	87,000	25,700	3,4:1
Tanks	950	232	4,1:1
Armoured Combat Vehicles	1,600	929	1,7:1
Artillery	1,000	3,005	1:3
Combat Aircraft	190	108	1,8:1

Source: Military Balance 1995/96, pp. 85–86, 118–119.

against Finland because of the need to protect Northern Fleet deployments in the Kola Peninsula, Helsinki can feel quite comfortable – even under the shadow of the huge Russian elephant.

The Finnish experience in the area of defence building shows that if national efforts are accompanied by arms control measures imposing limits on Russian arms deployments in border areas, even a small state is able to establish a credible national defence system without joining NATO or other military blocks.

In this respect, the Baltic States have plenty of room to build up national armed forces. During their first five years of independence, the Baltics have limited themselves by establishing small rifle units devoted to peacekeeping operations. However, if the Balts were really concerned with Russian aggression, they would instead be concentrating their efforts on such things as establishing their own air defences, deploying artillery, and, particularly, anti-tank weapons including helicopters.

Limited efforts made by the Baltic States in building up their own defences during the past five years indirectly indicates that they do not perceive the threat of near-term Russian aggression as being a realistic one. To some Moscow analysts, these actions, coupled with Baltic claims for the need to enter NATO as a precaution against Russian instability, seem quite incredible. From their viewpoint, the Baltics' abstinence from forces build up at the peak of Russia's domestic troubles in 1992–94 raises the legitimate question as to why the Balts are becoming so concerned now, especially when Russian democracy has reached relative stability?

There is not enough space in this Chapter to discuss all the potential fears Russia has related to the Baltics' possible incorporation into NATO. However, a few can be briefly listed here.

Moscow's main fear is connected to the fact that Baltic incorporation into NATO would bring the biggest military machine in the world too close to Russia's heartland. Based on Baltic airfields, supersonic aircrafts could reach Moscow in 20 minutes. It places key Russian command and control facilities under the threat of an effective disarming attack within a very short flight time. In scientific military terms, such capabilities are evaluated as being highly destabilising because they provoke the weaker side to inflict preemptive strikes in order to guarantee the survival of its most important defence infrastructure.

Since Moscow's political and military headquarters are important not only for commanding conventional troops, but nuclear as well, this pre-emption strategy would have to incorporate nuclear thinking. It creates the elevated risk that in the case of a major crisis in Russo-Western relations, Moscow could, under heavy pressure, launch pre-emptive attacks not only against military facilities on Baltic soil, but against targets in the United States as well. In the latter scenario, strategic nuclear forces would have to be used.

Thus, as a result of, say, riots in Russian-speaking cities like Narva or Daugavpils, the West could find itself risking a spontaneous escalation leading to an all-out nuclear Armageddon – all because of a relatively minor crisis.

The new strategic situation will place under question some important arms control agreements. Extreme vulnerability of Russia's heartland caused by a NATO military presence in the Baltic States would stimulate the Kremlin to pose symmetrical threats to major European capitals. Such retaliation could be carried out through the deployment of intermediate-range ballistic missiles with the ability to reach their targets within a period similar to the flight time of NATO supersonic bombers or fighters from the Baltic territory to Moscow. Since such missiles are currently prohibited by the INF Treaty signed by the Soviet Union and the United States in 1988, withdrawal from this Treaty would be necessary. In February 1996, Russian Minister of Foreign Affairs Yevgeny Primakov mentioned such a possibility as a potential countermeasure against NATO eastward expansion.

If Moscow's headquarters for Russian strategic nuclear forces is placed under the threat of a decapitating, short warning strike, the Russian military will subsequently face the need to increase alert status of the strategic forces to the shortest possible timeframe. It could damage the bilateral de-targeting agreements signed after the Cold War between Russia, the United States, Britain and France which determined that missiles of the four countries could no longer be targeted at each other's territories. The agreements led to a situation where if one needed to return missiles to "normal" targeting, some time would be allotted for transmitting targeting programs enabling the missiles to hit targets at adversarial soils. Under strong time pressures the military might decide not to risk and abandon the de-targeting mode in order to save several minutes or seconds.

Forward basing of NATO forces in the Baltic States would permit NATO to hit in European Russia deployed mobile single-warhead missiles, strategic bomber airfields and submarines at their bases. These are the types of weapons required by the START II Treaty. In order to provide credibility for its deterrent forces, Russia would have to return to silo based MIRVed ICBMs, weapons best suited for a quick launch on warning of an adversarial attack. However, these weapons are prohibited by START II and, therefore, might provide Moscow with a strong stimulus to withdraw from this important Treaty as well.

Baltic incorporation into NATO would mean that the Kaliningrad exclave would become completely encircled by NATO countries. In Moscow, this would certainly be perceived as an extraordinary threat to Russia's integrity and could very well stimulate higher military deployments – including nuclear weapons – in the oblast. Russia would also have to increase its contingencies in the North-western military district in order to protect Moscow and St. Petersburg from possible invasion.

Even the first wave of eastward expansion by NATO could provide strong incentive for Russia to establish preferential relations with Belarus in order to keep NATO forces as far as possible to the west of Moscow. Almost inevitably, Baltic incorporation into NATO would cause the modernising of Belarusian forces and the deployment of Russian troops in western Belarus. In case of war, they would have the task of de-blocking the Kaliningrad exclave and interrupting the ground communication lines necessary for reinforcing NATO troops deployed in the Baltic States.

This highlights the fact that the Baltic States can not be reliably protected by the West. Strategically, it would be an extremely difficult move for the United States to make its national territory a target for a spontaneous Russian nuclear attack based on something happening in Latgalia or North-eastern Estonia. The ratification of such arrangements in the US Senate would be quite problematic and hence, raises questions about the credibility of US guarantees to the Baltic States.

Certainly, to compensate for natural vulnerabilities, NATO could deploy a large number of troops on Baltic soil able to defend itself even if the corridor between Kaliningrad and Belarus should become interrupted for reinforcements from Poland. Baltic Sea communication lines could also become imperilled if Russia chooses to deploy large amounts of attack submarines, sea mines and naval aviation in the area. Given Russia's obvious geographic advantages for force reinforcements in such a situation, NATO forces in the Baltic States would remain vulnerable.

Such NATO deployments could only serve to increase Russian fears and, ultimately, lead to a further build up of Russian forces in the North-western military district and Belarus. It would also strengthen the incentive for a pre-emptive attack against the NATO troops in the Baltics.

It seems Baltic incorporation into NATO may leave the militaries of both sides with only two gloomy strategies: one, to inflict a disarming and decapitating strike against Russia in order to prevent a defeat of NATO troops in the Baltics at a later stage; and two, to pre-empt a NATO disarming strike by attacking and encircling NATO troops in the Baltics. Both scenarios, however, would most likely be accompanied by escalation to a nuclear level.

The present security environment offers the Baltic States a unique opportunity. For the first time in modern history, Russian military deployments in border areas have been reduced so considerably as to be comparable with the national forces of tiny Finland. If the Baltic States could find ways to achieve a security co-operation amongst themselves, they would certainly be able to build up forces of Finnish proportions and hence, command Western support.

Additionally, if the build up were to be followed by a co-operative approach to Russia, the Baltic States could realistically expect the number of Russian troops in their vicinity to be even less than it is now. Conversely, Russia could also choose to concentrate a larger number of troops in the region. However, this could just as easily be monitored by the West with a sufficient warning period to implement countermeasures.

This type of defence build up and arms control approach would, in military terms, provide a realistic direction for the enhancement of the Baltic States' security without formal incorporation into NATO. Conversely, the price for NATO membership may be seen as both: security guarantees which can not be perceived as reliable and credible; and the possibility of increased Russian military deployments around the Baltic States heightening the territory as a potential target for Russia's weapons (including weapons of mass destruction).

Some Baltic politicians believe that application for NATO membership provides a valuable political tool for deterring Russia's possible coercion. However, this would only be the case if the door is left open for the Balts to change their minds. Current Baltic policy, which under certain conditions bluntly rejects any options which could be considered alternative for their security, effectively deprives them the fruits of their NATO policy. In Russia's eyes, the Balts firm stance in desiring to enter NATO has effectively closed the door to negotiating a possible retreat from this position i.e., there is no reason to hold negotiations when one knows in advance that no concessions can be achieved. Instead, Moscow, in its attempt to block Baltic application, is forced to concentrate on talks with the West (not completely without success).

Ultimately, this has put the Baltic States in an awkward position they would have hoped to avoid: their future security is in the hands of outside powers (Russia and the West). Rather than direct negotiations with the Kremlin on attempts to reduce Russian threats and further the reduction of Russian forces and build up of confidence in border areas, Baltic capitals must rely on the results of negotiations without their participation. This predicament can be compared to what the Baltics faced during the beginning of World War II.

The United States, and the West in general, remain firmly committed to the independence of the Baltic States. However, they possess other interests which can only be promoted through a dialogue with Russia e.g., the future of further nuclear arms reductions, non-proliferation, and the situation in the Middle East and the Western Pacific to name a few. The Baltic question is not nearly as vital for the West as it is for Russia or, naturally, the Baltics themselves. In negotiations with Moscow, the West takes the Baltic issue into consideration within a broader scope of mutual concessions and benefits. Thus Russia, in offering concessions in areas unrelated to Baltic security, consequently "buys" Western reluctance in accepting the Balts into NATO.

In a direct dialogue with the Baltic States, Russia would not be able to use such tools as strategic arms control or missile technologies deliveries to Iran. If Moscow really believed, as a result of such dialogue, that the opportunity for the Baltic capitals to change their attitude towards NATO membership existed, it would certainly be ready to make far reaching concessions. Naturally, no one is in better position to know exactly what Russian concessions are needed than the Baltic States. Consequently, with Western support and in co-operation with Russia, no one could receive greater benefit from such a dialogue than the Baltic States.

From challenges to opportunities?

Late 1996-early 1997 brought certain long awaited hopes for a Baltic-Russian dialogue to begin. Among the reasons for this are:

1 The West, in recognising that it could not provide real security guarantees for the Baltic States by granting them NATO member-ship, began to more actively advise Russia and the Baltics to find

better 'modus vivendi' through direct dialogue. As a result, Estonia hinted at the possibility of settling their border dispute, and Latvia commenced thinking on the desirability of a Russian-Latvian summit. After gaining victory in parliamentary elections, the Lithuanian right-wing coalition moderated its rhetoric around Kaliningrad and the Russian transit there.

In turn, after the March 1997 Helsinki Summit with President Clinton, Boris Yeltsin not only offered the Baltic States Russian security guarantees, but in what certainly should have been met with warm acceptance in the Baltic capitals, hinted for the first time that Russo-Baltic relations should not just be determined by a question of Russian ethnic minorities in Estonia and Latvia.

2 By 1996, the halt of the Russian exodus from the Baltic States removed Russian concerns that it needed to resettle more than one million Russian-speakers from Estonia, Latvia and Lithuania. During the drive toward independence, many ethnic Russians and Russian-speakers successfully found their niche in Baltic societies, particularly in the fields of economics and finance. In the medium term, it increased the Russians' leverage in gaining civil rights there. Estonia and Latvia moved to avoid mass deportation of non-residents from their territory. Hopefully for the longer term, the new generation of Baltic people will be less committed to historical prejudices and, thus, more open to the idea of building multi-ethnic societies.

3 Despite all the mutual mistrust and misperceptions, economic ties between Russia and the Balts, in absolute terms, significantly expanded since 1991. It has helped to maintain a business community inherently interested in preserving a good Russo-Baltic relationship. In the longer run, it would also help to reshape the attitudes of the Baltic elites towards Russia.

4 Since 1991, Russia has demonstrated good behaviour towards the Balts: it has never used its predominance for defending its interests through coercion or sanctions. Despite strong dissatisfaction among Russian society to the plight of their compatriots civil rights situations in Estonia and Latvia, Moscow, on an official level, has consistently avoided provocative statements. Russia's self restraint over the past five plus years goes a long way in showing that a democratic Russia can be a much more desirable neighbour than the former Soviet Union.

5 In the military arena, Russia has sharply reduced and withdrawn its armed forces from the Baltic States within a relatively short period

of time. This withdrawal was not accompanied by a forces build up in territories attached to the Baltic States, namely Kaliningrad and the North-western military district. This move represents a sharp contrast from the Soviet policy of the late 1980s where an acceptance of troop withdrawals from Eastern Europe was followed up by a redeployment to the western part of the USSR.

6 The issue of NATO expansion has deeply affected the relationship between Russia and the West, calling into question the very opportunity of engaging Russia into a consortia of Western states. It has sent wrongful signals to Moscow, specifically: Russia's 'good' behaviour in the 1990s has led to the significant deterioration of its international position and, thus, has revitalised the old syndrome of perceiving the West as a source of threat to the very existence of the Russian state.

It seems the West has not assumed lessons of the past. As an example, after World War I, policies aimed at establishing a system of balances against Germany by imposing humiliating restrictions and conditions on Berlin led to the revitalization of the specific threat this policy was supposed to avoid. The Baltic States emerged among the main victims of such policy. Conversely, the post World War II strategy, aimed at integrating West Germany into a system of Western economic, political and military alliances has become a source of sustainable and lasting peace and stability in Europe, something it hardly enjoyed in the past. As a result of this policy, the Baltic States, together with other Soviet republics including Russia, were able to liberate.

The Baltic States are vitally interested in having Russia integrated into the West. Alternatively, this development would make the Baltics a front-line player in possible confrontations between Russia and the West. However, Russia, in its continued present weakness, would only become a much more dangerous neighbour.

For 50 years it has been the dream of the Baltic people to reinstitute an independence broken as a result of the Molotov-Ribbentrop pact. This is why it is completely understandable that in suddenly gaining this, they have attempted to re-establish all the details of the past, including even a name of one of their 1930s presidents. However, independence is not only the implementation of a dream. Its consolidation requires responsible foreign and domestic policy. Fifty years did not just disappear, and realities of the 1990s considerably differ from those of the 1930s. This era provides many more opportunities and, consequently, to lose them would be a huge mistake.

Judging the present environment through the prism of the 1930s is simply dangerous. And, it should be remembered, the 30's ended by 1939.

Notes

1 Population of Lithuania, Latvia and Estonia constitutes 3.7 million, 2.6 million, and 1.4 million people, respectively. Therefore, the aggregate population of the Baltic States is approximately 7.7 million. Population of the Russian Federation is 147.5 million inhabitants.

2 The Military Balance, 1995/96.

3 Pavel T. Podlesny, Problemy i perspektivy rossiisko-baltiiskikh otnoshenii vtoroi poloviny 90-kh godov (Problems and Prospects for the Russian-Baltic Relations in Late 1990s), A paper presented for the Carnegie Moscow Center Baltic Project, February 1997 (in Russian).

4 The Baltic Observer, No. 37, 1995.

5 Mezhdunarodnaia Zhinzn', 1996, January, No. 1, p. 44 (in Russian).

6 See Podlesny.

7 Vneshnyaia torgovlya, June 1996 (in Russian).

8 Nils Muiznieks, Ethnic Relations in Latvia: A Brief Overview, A paper presented for International Conference: "NATO and Baltic States: Quo Vadis?", October 1996, p. 1.

9 Voprosy prav cheloveka v Latviiskoi respublike, 1994, p. 996 (Problems of Human Rights in Latvia Republic, 1994, p. 6), Riga, December 1996 (in Russian), p. 12.

10 See Podlesny.

11 Opinion of the Latvian National Human Rights Office on Differences in Rights of Citizens and Persons without Lativan Citizenship, Latvian National Human Rights Office, Rige, 18 December 1996.

12 Voprosy prav cheloveka v Latviiskoi respublike, 1994, p. 6 (Problems of Human Rights in Latvian Republic, 1994, p. 6), Rige, December 1996 (in Russian), p. 12.

13 See Muiznieks, p. 1.

14 Rossiia v tsifrakh – Gosudarstvennyi komitet RF po statistike (Russia in figures – Russian State Committee for Statistics), M., 1996, p. 29 p. 1 (in Russian).

15 See Podlesny, p. 3.

16 Release of Press Service of the President of Russian Federation 1997 pp. 1–2, 5, Moscow, February 11, 1997, (in Russian).

17 On the Long-term Line of Russia Towards the Baltic States, Commentary of Latvian Ministry of Foreign Affairs, Riga, February 1997.

18 Cit. in: Leonid Vardomsky, Lyudmila Vorobyova, Alexandr Yershov, Kaliningradskaia oblast' Rossiiskoi Federatsii: problemy i perspektivy (Kaliningrad Oblast' of the Russian Federation: Problems and Prospects). Chapter 1 in: Kaliningradskaia oblast' – segodnya. zavtra (Kaliningrad

Oblast' – Today and Tomorrow), Research Reports of Moscow Carnegie Center, Issue Fifth, Carnegie Endowment for International Peace, M., Raduga Publishing House, 1995, p. 46.

19 Ibid., pp. 32 pp. 4.
20 Ibid., p. 36; Military Balance 1995/96, pp. 105, 118, 298.
21 Military Balance 1995/96, p. 298.
22 For history of CFE negotiations see Richard A. Falkenrath, Shaping Europe's Military Order. The Origins and Consequences of the CFE Treaty, The MIT Press, Cambridge, Mass., 1995.
23 Vardomsky et. al.
24 On the Long-term Line of Russia Towards the Baltic States, Commentary of Latvian Ministry of Foreign Affairs, Riga, February 1997, p. 2.

List of contributors

Dr. Mare Haab
Researcher, Institute of International and Social Studies, Tallinn, Estonia.

Dr. Peter van Ham
Professor, George C. Marshall European Centre for Security Studies, Garmisch, Germany.

Dr. Birthe Hansen
Associate Professor, University of Copenhagen, Denmark.

Professor Bertel Heurlin
Research Director, Danish Institute of International Affairs, Copenhagen, Denmark.

Dr. Lena Jonson
Senior Research Fellow, Swedish Institute of International Affairs, Stockholm, Sweden.

Dr. Stuart Kaufman
Associate Professor, University of Kentucky, USA.

Dr. Alexander A. Pikayev
Research Director, Centre for Geopolitical and Military Forecasts, Moscow, Russia.

Index

THE
REAL
WAR